Only in Myanmar!

About the book

Embark on a personal adventure with Martin Mehner, as he plunges deep down memory lane, uncovering a wealth of authentic and exciting travelling experiences, accrued from years of living in the beautiful and thrilling country of Myanmar. Find yourself lost in the attractive mystery of the South-East Asian nation, and become astounded by the incredible aspects of culture, diversity and history presented by Martin's tale. This isn't just a recollection, it's a sprawling resource of invaluable insights into the key travel destinations and activities that you will not find highlighted in mainstream guidebooks. Envelop yourself and absorb inspiration for your own travels to this deeply fascinating country.

About the author

Martin Mehner is a tried and tested adorer of Myanmar, having spent the majority of a six-year period of his life deeply involved in the country. He first visited Myanmar in 2010 and was immediately taken by the beauty and diversity that the nation offered. By 2013, he'd decided to take up residence in the country, along with his wife – a Myanmar national. As the next three years unraveled, Martin and his wife would come to run a boarding school for underprivileged children in Myitkyina, located within the remote Kachin State. It goes without saying that Martin has explored every corner of this incredible country and has built up an invaluable wealth of experience that he now wishes to share with the world.

Bibliographic information published by the Deutsche Nationalbibliothek:

The Deutsche Nationalbibliothek lists this publication in the Deutsche Nationalbibliografie; detailed bibliographic data is available on the internet: *http://dnb.dnb.de*

Publishing and print: BoD- Books on Demand, Norderstedt

ISBN: 978-3-7494-8535-2

Only in Myanmar!

Twelve unique experiences in the Golden
Country.

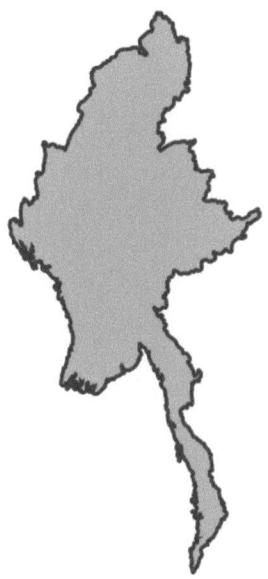

Martin Mehner

မင်္ဂလာပါ

Mingala Ba

Table of contents

1. Introduction

Dear reader,

Myanmar is a country that has often been in the news for all the wrong reasons: ethnic tensions, civil wars, natural disasters, poverty, and a military dictatorship. All this is associated with the country itself. And yet, the nation is so much more.

No country I have ever been to, has been as unique and at the same time as friendly and welcoming as Myanmar. Most Myanmar travelers I was allowed to meet, were just as overwhelmed by the experience as me. Many of them make regular returns, coming back year after year to spend more time there.

Although it might not always be comfortable, travelling to Myanmar is an experience you will most certainly never forget. Due to how globalized the world is today, and how every city or country is becoming increasingly more alike, standing out like Myanmar is something truly precious.

In many ways, it's a journey back in time, to a place that isn't just an artificially created tourist destination, but something much more authentic and real.

Not only that, Myanmar is incredibly diverse and offers sheer endless opportunities for exploration and discovery. In the south, you can find beautiful, untouched tropical beaches, which you'll have all to yourself: kilometers of silver sand and turquoise water, without hotels, restaurants or any other infrastructure to taint it. In the north you can go on trekking tours through the virtually uninhabited Himalayan foothills and explore breathtaking, untouched nature. In the cultural and economic capital of Yangon, you can go sightseeing and enjoy the city with the highest density of colonial buildings in all South-East Asia. In Bagan, you can explore over 2200 pagodas dating from the 9th to 13th century. And finally, in Shan State, you can visit Inle Lake, with its swimming gardens, magnificent pagodas and a variety of tribal cultures. No matter what interests you may have, Myanmar has a lot to offer if you are open-minded, and willing to give the country a fair chance.

For me, Myanmar has been an essential part of my life for a while now. It was the final country I visited on my South-East Asian journey in 2010 but impacted me like no other. It was just so different to everything I had previously seen and experienced. I went from being a naive, unsuspecting first-time visitor to an actual Myanmar regular. I got married to my wife that I was so lucky to have met during my first visit, and in 2013 I started to live permanently in the "Golden Country". Two years later, my son was born in Myitkyina, the capital of Kachin state and the place I would call home for around three years. It certainly wouldn`t be an exaggeration to say that I am deeply and profoundly connected to Myanmar.

I have undergone a plethora of fantastic experiences during my time in Myanmar, and I'm eager to share some of the best ones with you. You will likely read this book because you are planning your first visit to

Myanmar, or maybe you've already fallen in love with the country and have decided you want to come back for more. Throughout this book, I will mainly focus on travel-related experiences, in which Myanmar is truly like no other country.

What could be more exciting than highlighting some of the experiences that are especially unique and perhaps only to be found here? I hope you find some of the adventures I describe interesting and maybe even want to try them out for yourself. It would be fantastic for me if some of the chapters of this book can inspire you in your travels. I have personally experienced all the places and activities I write about, and I hope you can feel this authenticity and passion when reading.

I want this book to be a tool that you can use to get the most out of your Myanmar travels. For this reason, I have compiled a collection of some of the best travel-related books and websites. If you find one of the experiences I write about inspiring, you can also use these sources to get some more detailed information and read on.

Please keep in mind that I am not a professional writer; I am not even a native English speaker. This book is not a well-calculated travel book but a project of my heart.

Since I left Myanmar, I've often found myself reminiscing about the country and all that belongs to it. That's the reason why I've decided to recapture some of the greatest experiences I had when I lived there. The truth is that writing this book and recollecting my memories was often a more bittersweet experience than I expected it to be. It was a joy to write about something I love and share it with you, but at the same time, it was also sometimes painful. It made me realize just how much I miss being there.

Yours sincerely,

Martin Mehner

2. The Train: An Unforgettable 24-Hour Journey

One of the most memorable experiences I had in Myanmar was taking the long-distance train from Mandalay to Myitkyina.

Train rides can't be too much of a challenge, right? Think again. To get from Mandalay to Myitkyina you will have to travel 550 km, which doesn't sound like that much, but due to how slow the train moves, and the constant stops, it takes anywhere from 21 to 25 hours. That's assuming nothing goes wrong, of course. But what could possibly go wrong? The railway carriage and locomotive are from colonial times, and are far from reliable, or well maintained. The tracks are incredibly rebellious, and from time to time, you will struggle to stay in your seat because of how much the train bucks up and down.

Calling it bumpy is an absolute understatement. It´s often entertaining when the constant shaking finally frees the bags you stored in the overhead compartment, and they come to say hello to your head. Of course, this is also going to happen right after you've finally managed to cry yourself to sleep.

Worst of all are the passenger cabins, which you're not just sharing with other people. No one wants to be alone, so an ever-social selection of bugs, flies, cockroaches and mosquitoes will keep you company during the night.

Air conditioning, western toilets, or cleanliness? Don't even ask. Sounds like fun, right?

If you happen to take one of the three to four daily trains that run from Mandalay to Myitkyina your journey is going to start in Mandalay´s schizophrenic train station. A huge 7-floor concrete building that serves as one of the main transport hubs, right in the middle of the country. It looks somewhat decent from the outside, yet it only takes a few steps inside of it to realize that it's not even close to what you might have hoped it would be.

You might have been prepared for the betel nut strains everywhere, you are used to the rubbish, and yes, you know it can be overcrowded, but the thing that is really going to bother you is that even after ten minutes of walking around, you still have no clue where the damn ticket counter for foreign travelers is. It's okay, just interpret the walk around the train station as a brief sightseeing tour.

Once you've found the ticket counter, things are going to be easy, right? Erm… I am sorry, they won't. It's Myanmar. Here is what is going to go wrong: the ticket officer is currently drinking tea and watching Myanmar Idol at the local teashop, and no one else has the authority to issue tickets to foreign travelers; the train you want to take is already fully booked; you forgot to bring passport copies; you don't have the exact amount of US dollars needed to buy the ticket, and the ticket counter has no change. To top it all off, you could get a real Myanmar specialty: one of your bills gets rejected because it's not crisp enough. Hey, no one said it's going to be easy.

A couple of days later, you're finally going to embark on the train journey of your life. I am serious about this: the enjoyable, and the miserable aspects of this train ride are almost certain to make it the most memorable journey you will ever experience.

With a mix of worry about what awaits you and a sense of adventure and curiosity, you return to Mandalay´s central train station, ready to board the train. However, nothing is easy in Myanmar, you already know that. Finding the right platform isn't hard but when looking at the ticket and wondering which railcar you have to go to, you are going to realize that all the numbers used are in Myanmar. This is when you know you should have learned some Myanmar language before the trip.

It's too late for that now, but hey, you are going to end up in the right seat eventually, right? In Myanmar, things always have a way of magically working out in the end. The most important thing, as usual, is to not stress out and stay relaxed. Just show one of the guys in uniform where your seat is if you can't find it alone. The people all over the country are usually incredibly helpful and will try their best to make sure you are okay. It doesn't matter if it's the staff of Myanmar Railways or just the regular people you meet in everyday life.

Once the train starts rolling, the only thing left for you to do is to sit down and be patient. Just as I did, you will likely feel a sense of relief when realize you've made it to the correct seat in time, with your bag being semi-safely stored and being prepared for the trip ahead. Once you've left Mandalay, you will cross the mighty Ayeyarwaddy river via the Inwa bridge and have a great chance to snatch few final glimpses of the beautiful pagoda covered hills of Sagaing. Once these views have passed, little more will stand out. None of the towns you pass on the way are remarkable, be it Shwebo, Zigon or Kawlin. One train station blurs into another, and you zip past endless rice-fields, or a few nondescript hills.

But this is not a train you take for the scenic views. It's about the experience, and that comes in droves. Once you've passed the first few hours, you will realize that the train tracks really are deteriorated everywhere, and it wasn't just a rough patch you went through. One thing that is truly unique and can be found *Only in Myanmar*, is that some people there call their trains 'discos'. And I have to agree: you get to meet a lot of people, and the constant shaking sure makes for an exciting dance. Not even convinced non-dancers like me can resist it. Just a little reminder to make you more enthusiastic about the whole experience: Kantbalu, one of the towns on the way, was the scene of a deadly train accident in 2012. Several wagons carrying diesel and gasoline derailed and burned, and a total of 27 people died, with over 80 people being injured. According to news reports, many of the deaths and injuries were due to people trying to scavenge the spilled gasoline and diesel.

Thanks to the never-ending supply of vendors that pass through the trains, it seems that there is literally nothing you could have forgotten to buy before the trip. Water and all kinds of beverages commonly found in Myanmar? Check. Fruits, fried snacks, noodle dishes, rice and curry? Check. Sanitary items like toilet paper, soap, tissue? Check. Pain killers, nasal inhalers for a running nose, alternative (natural) medicine? Check. Everything is a little more expensive compared to regular shops, and the food is usually not quite as tasty, but there's a pretty good supply of everything you could possibly need.

But there is also a downside to this steady flow of goods. As you might imagine, there are not enough rubbish bins on the train, and when people eat, some of the food is going to end up on the seats or on the floor of the railcar. The longer the train ride goes, the dirtier it gets. On top of that, the Myanmar railway workers probably don't do the most thorough cleaning job in the world after the train has come to its final stop in Myitkyina. And who can blame them? It can also be quite a shock for western travelers to see how people throw the remains of their dishes, empty beverage cans, water bottles, tissues, plastic bags etc. out of the window of the train. It's certainly not a very environmentally friendly way to dispose of trash. Then again, what options are there? Keep the rubbish in the train and waddle through heaps of waste by the end of the ride? Doesn't sound like a great plan to me. I remain hopeful that, as with everything, this is going to change in the future, and the Myanmar Railway is going to find ways to make sure everything gets cleaned effectively.

No matter how long the train ride might feel, remember that this is a great chance to observe how regular people in Myanmar live. It doesn't matter if it's your fellow passengers, the ticket officers, the vendors in the train, the people in the train stations or even the farmers working in the fields you pass through. Many people travel so they can get an authentic experience of what life is like in foreign countries. A train ride through Myanmar is just that. Furthermore, with all the time you have and the lack of useful internet you won't be too distracted by your phone either. Finally, some time to pay attention to what is going on in the world around you.

Nansiaung is the first town you pass through once you have crossed the inconspicuous border from Sagaing Division into the ominous Kachin state, one of Myanmar's least travelled regions. It's the notorious home of not just one but several armed rebel groups who, despite the takeover by Aung San Suu Kyi, remain at war with the Tatmadaw, Myanmar's armed forces. But don't worry, Kachin state is a relatively safe place for travelers. All the areas around the main towns are secure, and the government is very cautious not to let any tourists go into more remote areas, which could potentially be home to dangerous battle zones. Neither the rebel forces nor the government authorities pose a threat to you.

The positive side of this is of course that unlike Bagan, Inle Lake, Ngapali and the other popular tourist hotspots Kachin state is almost totally unspoilt by tourism. Kachin state is also known for being the home of the infamous jade mines in Hpakant, where the world's best jadeite is being mined, and tens of thousands of people from all over Myanmar seek to strike a fortune. Unfortunately, Hpakant is one of the areas of Kachin state that tourists, for now, are not allowed to go to. Despite all these interesting aspects of travel to Kachin state you probably will not notice too much of a difference between the towns you passed through in Sagaing Division, and the villages you pass through now. At first glance, everything looks pretty much the same.

Arriving in Kachin state also means that by now you have already covered around 400km – you're more than halfway there! Time for a good night's rest. It's too bad that by now the railcar has been taken over by millions of insects, mainly bugs, flies and mosquitos. The light bulbs of the wagons are the perfect meeting points for all the insects that soar around Myanmar´s warm night air. The sight of swarms of insects in your railcar is not something that helps you find any sleep, but fears of being bitten to death or having thousands of bugs in your hair and clothes are mostly unfounded. Fortunately, your new travel companion's obsession with light means that you will mostly be left alone, free to take a good nap. To be honest, I was probably bitten more in the hotel rooms with bad or missing mosquito nets than on Myanmar's trains. Buying some repellent is still a good idea, though.

It's time to discuss something else that I know you're very worried about, so let's get it over with. The toilets. For many, this is going to be the biggest worry about the ride. It doesn't matter which class you are travelling in, the toilets in the trains are basically just a 2m² room with a hole in the ground and a water bucket to clean up the mess. There are sometimes small washbasins outside the toilet, but they don't always work. What makes using these toilets really challenging is the constant shaking of the train, as you could imagine. It can almost become impossible to use a bathroom properly when you're struggling to stay on your feet. When you are going through a rough stretch with particularly adverse track conditions, it's probably better to wait a few minutes and delay the inevitable toilet experience some more. The only thing left to write about the whole thing is perhaps just a heartfelt "good luck". Oh, and no matter what happens, remember there is always more water and soap!

If you are lucky enough and the train didn't break down due to mechanical problems and didn't derail, you will eventually make it to Myitkyina after around 24 hours. The feeling of finally arriving after half an eternity on a train is fantastic! Once you've made it to Myitkyina, you will have a good choice of places in which you can have the most refreshing shower of your life. There are cheap guesthouses like the YMCA, mid-range options like Hotel Madira or even a luxurious hotel called "Palm Springs Resort" with a beautiful pool overlooking the mighty Ayeyarwaddy River.

Trust me, showering after 24 hours on a Myanmar train is genuinely a marvelous feeling. Getting rid of all the sweat and dust and putting on some fresh clothes is fantastic. Not just for you, but the people around you will thank you too! When in Myitkyina, don't forget to take a nice, long walk along the banks of the mighty Ayeyarwaddy and visit the night market (5-8 pm) where you can taste some delicious food. A day trip to Myitsone is also a must when in Myitkyina. This place is where the Malikha river and the Nmaikha river meet and the mighty Ayeyarwaddy is born. A small boat tour around the confluence should not be missed.

Unfortunately, the recent boom in gold mining has made the water look a lot muddier than it used to be. There are also some small-scale artisan gold mining sights around the confluence; if you are interested, you can look at how gold is mined here. Of course, there are also plenty of restaurants at Myitsone. Considering the gold mining industry, I would advise you to not eat any fish caught in the river. The concentration of mercury and cyanide is likely everything but healthy. This also applies to fish in Myitkyina or further downstream.

If you decide that the 24-hour train to Myitkyina is a bit too hardcore for you there is also the more scenic (and touristy) train line into the hills of Shan state. It starts in Mandalay and goes all the way to Lashio. On this route you will also come across one of the most commonly photographed places in all of Myanmar, the Goteik Viaduct. It was constructed in 1899 to increase the British empire's control over Myanmar. The total height tops out at around 100 meters and isn't for the faint of heart.

Last but certainly not least, I have some tips to make it easier for you to get through this arduous trip. One of the most important things to keep in mind is that you'll need warm clothes if you travel during the colder months of the year (November-April). The further north you reach, the colder it gets. The nights in Kachin state can be uncomfortably cold with temperatures going down to around 6-7°C. There can even be snow in some villages at higher altitudes. The constant breeze that gets into the trains through the windows exacerbates the problem further. Make sure to bring a blanket and a warm jacket.

Always make sure you have enough water and soap to wash your hands, and toilet paper to clean up everything else. You can get these items from the mentioned vendors, but it's good to stock up to make sure you are covered for possible emergencies. If you aren't used to Myanmar street-food or if you tend to get an upset stomach, it's also advisable to hold back on the food that gets sold in the train. To make sure you don't get food-sick you can bring some food from a reliable source in Mandalay when you board the train. As I mentioned before, the food sold in trains is usually not quite as tasty and cheap as the food elsewhere. You will not miss anything special by skipping the train food. Also, when buying a ticket, make sure you bring copies of your passport and visa. The ticket offices also often don't have change so try to bring lots of small US dollar bills. No matter what happens, stay calm, be friendly, and trust that things will get better soon.

3. Eat Fish Soup for Breakfast.

What better way to start the day than having some delicious fish soup! Yes, you just read that right; forget your croissants, your full English breakfast, your bread rolls, cornflakes, porridge, or whatever else you might like to have for breakfast. They don't stand a chance against the mighty Mohinga: Myanmar's national dish, and an absolute favorite for breakfast around the country. No matter where you are, you can be sure Mohinga is right there, waiting to help you kickstart your day.

One thing that is consistently lacking throughout many low to mid-range hotels and guesthouses in Myanmar is the breakfast they serve. Commonly, in the less touristic areas, the usual breakfast consists of toast, fried eggs, jam, horrible margarine and artificial orange juice. You will find having breakfast in a Myanmar guesthouse is acceptable once or twice, but soon after, it will become boring and much harder to stomach. You can eat a better version of this breakfast at home and missing out on the various Myanmar breakfast options is just not worth it. The breakfast itself is usually included in the room rate, so you can go and give it a try at no extra cost. Just head out to find a real Myanmar breakfast afterwards if what is served in your hotel doesn't excite you. Trust me, apart from a few guesthouses that have stepped up their breakfast game in recent years, it likely won't.

Unless your hotel is in a remote area, you are pretty much guaranteed to find a Mohinga street stall within minutes of leaving your room. If you are new to the area and aren't sure where to go, just try to figure out which places are popular with locals and go there. If you see people eating a brownish, noodle-based dish from bowls, there is a good chance you have found a Mohinga shop – congratulations! Many of the street shops use small plastic chairs that you would only use for children in the west. It's a bit odd for us westerners to see grown adults sitting on baby chairs, but I guess they are used because they are cheaper and easier to carry around; essential factors for running a small, mobile food stall. You might think of them as an equivalent to a poser table used by food stalls in western countries. Fear not, for despite their size, they are quite sturdy. I've never had one break down from carrying my not-so-small bum.

Understandably, trying out fish soup for breakfast might not sound like a very appealing idea to you. My mother would not even consider it when she visited me in Myanmar. The thought of having fish soup was too much for her to even dare try it out. But don't be hesitant, as Mohinga is nothing like the classic fish soup you would expect to get served in the west. If you weren't told that there is fish in Mohinga, you might not even notice that it's an actual fish soup. It doesn't smell like fish and is mild in taste.

So, what goes into your Mohinga? The essential ingredients are the vermicelli noodles that are cooked separately, which go into the bowl first. After that, a ladle of the actual soup gets poured over the noodles. This soup is the exciting part. Aside from the usual ingredients like onions, garlic and fish paste, toasted rice is added. This ingredient makes the soup much thicker. Depending on the availability, different types of fish can be used for Mohinga. The most classic Mohinga recipes, however, use catfish. One thing many people wonder about when trying out Mohinga for the first time is where the actual fish is. The answer is simple: it's in the soup. The reason why there aren't any big pieces of fish in it is because the fish gets separated from the fishbones and is mashed into a paste. This is the reason why you likely can't recognize it when eating the delicious Mohinga. Lemongrass is also often added to Mohinga, which services to counteract the initial fishiness of the soup.

Once the noodles and the soup are in the bowl, a variety of toppings are added on top. These vary from region to region but often include fried fritters, boiled eggs and fried onions. Some people also like their Mohinga to be spicy and will add chili to it. Try it out if you love spicy food – you won't be disappointed. The original recipe, however, is very mild. It's also very common to add some fresh lime juice; this is one thing I would always go for because it makes the dish taste fresh and light.

After you have tried Mohinga, you will understand why it is such a popular dish in Myanmar. It's not just delicious but also ideally suited as a regular breakfast meal. Unlike most of the fried snacks you can order at the teashops, it's not particularly heavy. Yet, it's filling and gives you enough energy to start a day full of exploring and sight-seeing. It's also a very economical breakfast, as depending on where you eat Mohinga it can be as cheap as 300 Kyats for one serving. Granted, prices have increased in recent years, but a serving of Mohinga and a coffee should still be available for less than 1000 Kyats. But the low prices don't mean Mohinga is a breakfast fit only for a poor man. Everyone in Myanmar loves Mohinga, whether they're rich, poor or something in between. It doesn't matter. Even though

Mohinga is most commonly eaten for breakfast, it isn't just a breakfast dish either. Many of the hawkers and street stalls sell it throughout the day. If you happen to get hungry in between lunch and dinner, a serving of Mohinga can always be found.

4. The Waterfall: An Adventure Through Remote Kachin State.

If you ever make it up to Myitkyina, the capital of Kachin state, one of the most exciting and adventurous day trips you can take is to a waterfall locally known as Sa Done Yei Dan Kone. It´s located east of the Ayeyarwaddy River, between Wainmaw and a village called Sa Done. The road connecting Wainmaw and the Chinese border was built by the same Chinese company that is developing the Myitsone hydropower dam. Needless to say, it´s in much better shape than almost any overland road you can find in Myanmar.

To make it to the waterfall, you will need to spend around 2 to 3 hours travelling from Myitkyina. The Sa Done waterfall is a charming destination for daytrips and you can even swim in some of its basins. But this trip is fantastic for bearing witness to the scenery you see on your journey, and the sense of adventure that travelling in such remote, untouched areas of the world gives you. The road winds its way through beautiful hill country. At some points along the way, you can also have a vast, unobstructed view over broad swathes of entirely undeveloped land.

However, the trip is not just exciting because of the scenery. Kachin state is one of the areas of Myanmar that is still suffering from an armed conflict: this is the reason you will see plenty of military outposts and Tatmadaw personnel on the way. But don't worry, even though it might sound dangerous, it's actually completely safe. If it weren't, you wouldn't be able to make it there anyway, as in unsafe situations, the police or the military will create checkpoints, and not let any tourists through. You can say what you want about the travel restrictions, but one thing is for sure: you'd have to try very hard to get into trouble in Myanmar.

The first thing you will have to do to get this adventure started is to rent a motorbike in Myitkyina. If your hotel or guesthouse can't help you with that, you can go and visit the YMCA and ask there. They will be able to help you. For day trips to Sa Done Yei Dan Kone, I have the same essential advice that I have for trips around Dawei's beaches: only hop on a motorbike if you are a somewhat competent rider; check your bike thoroughly before getting started, and always wear a helmet. I have lived in Myitkyina for around three years, and helmet controls have gotten increasingly frequent. If you want to avoid getting into trouble, and of course if you want to remain safe, don't ride without a helmet. Riding around Myitkyina's city center is challenging. The streets are usually packed with motorbikes and cars that can often be found speeding. I do not recommend using a bike for short trips that can otherwise be made on foot. The risk of having an accident is considerable for someone who isn't used to riding motorbikes in Myanmar.

That being said, once you've left Myitkyina, the traffic becomes easier to deal with. At first, you will be heading north towards the gigantic Ba La Min Than bridge. This bridge is situated at the northern edge of the city and offers excellent views. I recommend riding across the bridge and then stopping at the small pagoda right next to it on the bank of the Ayeyarwaddy River. The pagoda itself is not very interesting, but the views across the mighty river are magnificent. Don't miss this spot. It's fascinating to watch the gigantic river wind its way south. It's almost like you can feel the natural power of these enormous amounts of water, thrashing and flowing along their course.

After a few more kilometers on the main highway, you will make it to Waingmaw. At the main intersection of the town you will have to turn left and head east towards the Chinese border. Once you've left the center of Waingmaw, you will drive past a staggering number of Christian (mainly Baptist) churches and bible schools. From here it takes around 15 minutes to arrive at Washawng, the last town before heading out deeper into the hills. Washawng is home to a small dam, and plenty of day-trippers come here to enjoy the (not so picturesque) river and reservoir. It´s worth a short stop even though it's far from remarkable. Washawng is an excellent place to stock up on some food and drinks for your onward journey. If you have any doubts about the condition of your motorbike, you should use one of the workshops along the road; worrying about your bike breaking down will spoil your trip, so it's a good idea to get some peace of mind. Also, make sure you fill up your fuel tank because there aren't that many gasoline shops along the way.

Shortly after the dam, the Chinese portion of the road starts. Once you are on the Chinese road, it's as though you leave the regular Myanmar behind and enter a completely different world. The contrast is truly remarkable. The flatlands of the Ayeyarwaddy are replaced with rolling hill country. There are no more churches or villages along the now-winding roads. The usual stream of motorbikes and cars you see in Myitkyina and Waingmaw dwindles and is replaced by a smaller count of cars, bustling together on their way to the Chinese border, as well as there being Chinese trucks and Tatmadaw vehicles. The traffic is generally light, and it's nothing compared to the number of vehicles on the main highway from Myitkyina to Waingmaw. The beautiful rolling hills, fine road conditions and lighter traffic make this road a heaven for any motorbike lover. If I had the opportunity to select a road for a few hours of motorbike riding, I would not hesitate to choose this road over any other I have experienced on my travels. When I lived in Myitkyina, I regularly took my bikes here for some fun. The joy of riding on this fantastic road combined with the vulnerability of riding a motorbike in such a remote and underdeveloped area made it an adventure every single time. It isn't a very relaxing thought to think about how far the next medical "facilities" are away if something does go wrong. This aspect only compounds the sensation of adventure, adding a thrilling perspective to an already exciting journey.

The first few kilometers after leaving Washawng are mostly uphill. There aren't many options when renting motorbikes in Myitkyina, and you will most likely end up on a small, Chinese 125cc step-through. The little air-cooled engines don't like to get pushed too hard when having to carry a heavy westerner up the hills. So, take it slow and just do you and your bike a favor by enjoying the scenery, instead of trying to go fast. It will take around 90 minutes to reach the waterfall from Washawng so taking a break every now and then is a must. The seat of your Chinese pocket rocket will be mighty uncomfortable after the first few kilometers. It's an unfortunate fact that the ergonomics of your typical Chinese step-through bike are just not right for bigger people. Everything is too small and cramped. Hopefully there will be more options for motorbike rentals in the future.

Every so often, you will see water hoses along the road. Initially, it might not be apparent to you what they are used for, but after a while you will figure out that many people in Myanmar use them to cool down the engines of their bikes and cars. They can be found along any road that traverses steep hills. Of course, this seems very strange to us because the energy released by pouring cold water on a hot engine can cause cracks and deformations. Instead of doing your vehicle a favor, you will create more issues. It seems as though it will take some time until people in Myanmar realize that this habit is actually causing harm.

Another exciting thing about the road is the military presence you will see along the way. Every few kilometers there is an army outpost with some stationed Tatmadaw personal. There are usually also guards on the bridges. This is mainly because the road is considered a vital aspect of the infrastructure that enables trade with China, and the Kachin Independence Army has been known to target such infrastructure to follow their political agenda. Even though it might sound dangerous, the road is generally safe to use. As mentioned before, if there are any problems, you will be stopped long before you can get yourself into trouble. I have been to the Sa Done Yei Dan Kone regularly while living in Myitkyina and never had any problem.
Understandably, seeing soldiers might scare some travelers; we all know how bad the reputation of Myanmar's military is. The truth is that any contact I had with the soldiers stationed on this road were always amicable. These guys are not the monsters some media outlets would want you to believe. Give them a smile or

a wink, and you will see they are just as friendly as everyone else in Myanmar. Another plus is that I have never seen any checkpoints on the way, so in this sense your adventure is likely going to be completely hassle-free.

After around 90 minutes, you will reach a bridge that stretches across a beautiful creek. Depending on the season you travel in it's either a small trickle of water along the beautiful white rocks or a massive, flowing stream. When you spot this creek, you'll know that you have finally made it! Right after the bridge, there are a few houses, as well as several restaurants. There is also a small police outpost there, and on the right side of the road is a shaded parking spot for your bike. From here, a path goes down to a bridge that will bring you right back over the same creek you just passed on your bike. The hike to the waterfall only takes a few minutes, so don't worry about having to walk too far. In the parking area is a signboard about the Sa Done Yei Dan Kone. Officially there is a 3 USD entrance fee for foreigners, but from my experience this isn't enforced at all. The only thing you pay is around 200 Kyats for the motorbike parking.

The prominent basin a few meters uphill is a beautiful place for a refreshing bath. The water is nice and cold, and very inviting after hours of uncomfortable travel on the road. There are usually some day-trippers around, but if you are lucky, you might have the entire waterfall to yourself. Admittedly, it's not the Niagara Falls, but the creek with its white rocks, the waterfall and its basins, the jungles of the Kachin hills and the sense of adventure still make for an impressive combination.

By the time you arrive at the waterfall, you will be hungry for sure. The restaurants next to the waterfall are very decent, considering how remote they are. They are owned by Chinese-Myanmar families and cater to the many people passing by on their way to China. They serve tasty curries and rice. When I was there, I always went for the dried meat they make on-site. It's delicious, so if you see it, just go for it. The only downside is that it's often dried next to the road, so you are sure to get plenty of pollutants from all the big, diesel engines powering the Chinese trucks up the hills. Who knows, maybe it's the smoke of the diesels that give it that delicious smoke-dried aroma - just ignore the worries and enjoy. A pretty neat idea is to buy some food at the restaurants and take it with you to the waterfall. The Myanmar term for takeaway food is "pah-sel". As you can probably guess, it's derived from the English word parcel. If you say it everyone will know you want to take the food with you. Next to the basins of the waterfall, there are some huts made of wood and bamboo. They serve as an excellent place for a picnic. Just make sure you take all the rubbish with you when you leave. As anywhere in Myanmar, many visitors don't have much awareness about pollution. They often leave empty beverage cans, Styrofoam boxes and plastic bags behind when leaving the waterfall.

I recommend spending at least two hours at the waterfall before heading back. Passing some time there is the only way for your butt to recover, and to get your limbs ready for another uncomfortable ride on your bike. It's quite easy to occupy a few hours there anyway, as you can swim, relax, have some food or even take a small nap. Just don't get bitten by a snake. I am not trying to worry you, but I have seen a pretty scary looking snake at the waterfall once.

Considering how long it takes to get back to Myitkyina, I recommend leaving before 3pm to avoid riding in the dark. Myanmar´s roads are dangerous enough during the day and getting help in case of an accident or a mechanical issue is way harder in the dark. The best back-up plan for when something goes majorly wrong with your bike is to try to flag down one of the passing trucks and see if they can help you by transporting you and the bike back to Myitkyina. It's Myanmar, and most people will be keen to help you out. There is no need to panic if something does go wrong. Living in Myanmar for three years taught me that everything is going to work out in the end, no matter how bad the situation seems. Never forget to ride carefully; the risk of having an accident is the thing you should be worried about most.

5. Visit a Myanmar Beer Bar.

Beer bars, or 'beer stations', as they are called in Myanmar, often don't get enough recognition by foreign tourists. I'm aware this book is called "Only in Myanmar!" and you are right - beer bars can be found in most countries. The ones in Myanmar, however, are truly unique, and are well worth a visit or two. They are nothing like the 'girly' beer bars you would find in Thailand or Cambodia, and could be best compared to traditional British pubs. The only significant difference between British and Myanmar 'pubs' is off course that they don't serve decent food in England. The beer bars in Myanmar are very basic in appearance; almost unassuming, but don't let the simplicity fool you into thinking they are only suited for people that are after cheap booze. The truth is they are far from that. If you're not familiar with these venues and are worried about having to deal with drunk or misbehaving men, allow me to reassure you: I have rarely (if ever) experienced anti-social behavior from Myanmar men at beer bars. Even while drunk, they seem to retain their polite respectfulness toward others, which is undoubtedly another significant improvement over British pubs. I guess being in a bar full of well-behaved drunkards is another phenomenon found *Only in Myanmar*!

One of the main differences to the beer bars in other countries is that their Myanmar counterparts also serve a wide variety of foods. All the regular curries that you will be served in traditional Myanmar restaurants can be found in many beer stalls too. It wouldn't be fair to assume that the beer shops generally have worse tasting curries either. The truth is that no matter if you go to a regular restaurant or a beer shop, there will be both good and bad experiences. This is another aspect that I find to be unique about Myanmar food: although most restaurants look somewhat similar from the outside, the tastiness of the curries prepared by the cooks varies to an incredible degree. There isn't much consistency from place to place, and you never really know what you are going to get. Sure, to some degree, this applies to any country, but in Myanmar, it really is key to know your spots. For a traveler that is just passing through, this can be very frustrating because it's impossible to know the best places to eat without trying them all out by yourself.

One thing that sets the beer stations apart from the regular restaurants is that they often have a mouth-watering selection of juicy meats and vegetables that you can get served directly off the sizzling grill. Just point your finger at what you want, and voila, it will arrive at your table a few minutes later. The variation of meats and fish is usually quite impressive, because unlike western countries, people in Myanmar people still have a taste for livers, kidneys and other organs. Alternatively, you can also try out roasted chicken feet and pork fat (I heard it's good for your heart?) or pig tongue. Personally, I don't find any of that tasty, but opinions vary, and it may just be your thing. It isn't just meat and fish, of course. Try out the various types of barbequed eggs, for example. Or taste the delicious vegetables available - usually corn, okra, sugar snap peas and potatoes. The staff serves all the barbequed dishes with delicious, homemade chili and tamarind sauces with lime. At some of the smaller beer restaurants, however, you will have to make do with the standard bottled sauce you can find in stores and supermarkets.

If you come for the beer itself, you will also not be disappointed. There is always a selection of beer available on tap. How big this selection is, simply depends on the size of the beer shop. Most of them are local brands like Myanmar Beer, Dagon, and Andaman Gold. There are so many different beers available in Myanmar now, that it's hard to keep track of them all. Most of them are enjoyable, just don't expect them to be the culinary highlight of the trip. It would be a shame to miss the chance of trying all of them out – this line makes for a perfect excuse for beer lovers who need a reason to justify their consumption. Definitely a good aspect of the wide variety of local beers. I just hope your wife is more understanding than mine. She is immune to this sort of explanations. Well, I guess there's no beer for me then.

If you don't like the local beers, you can also fall back on the more familiar foreign beers. Many brands are becoming increasingly easier to find. While carrying out the research for this book, I came across some exciting news regarding the opening of Myanmar's first microbrewery in 2017, which produces a craft beer called "Burbrit" (a charming portmanteau of Burma and Britain). Unfortunately, I haven't had the chance to try it out because my time in Myanmar ended a year before that. Just in theory of course, as my wife wouldn't have allowed it anyway. She doesn't care about how elaborate a beer's brewing process is, or how fancy its name might sound.

Another reason to come to the beer shops are soccer matches. People in Myanmar love soccer and are avid fans of the English Premier League. Many of them have their favorite teams that they cheer for every weekend. A giveaway of this fact would be the sight of all the (albeit fake) Chelsea, Liverpool and Manchester United jerseys you see in the streets. Almost every beer shop has at least one or two big TVs used to broadcast the matches. Many even have signboards in front of their establishment that inform about the broadcasting schedule of the day. Granted, Myanmar beer shops aren't going to be offering the best public viewing quality but hey, it's better than nothing if you don't want to miss out on your regular dose of soccer.

Good food, cheap, plentiful beer, and soccer all in one place? How can you say no to that? These aspects are well-known and popular tastes for the local men (I guess we're the same worldwide) and the beer bars become packed in the evenings. It's only during the initial opening times in the afternoon that they don't have a huge number of customers. When prestigious soccer games are on, during the World Cup or when the Myanmar national team is playing, for example, the beer shops will always be open. It doesn't matter if it's evening, late night or early morning. These beer shops are a staple in every town; it would be unthinkable to imagine the streets of Myanmar without them. In that sense they are a little like the teashops of the evenings. Both the teashops and the beer shops are more than just a place to eat and drink. They are meeting points for friends, places to hang out and relax and places to discuss politics, work, sports and anything else. You might find them to be a bit too busy and chaotic for a proper dinner but at least try them out once when you come to Myanmar.

6. The Pagoda: An Arduous Climb

The pagodas are undoubtedly the main attractions in many areas of Myanmar. They come in all shapes and forms; some are gigantic and magnificent, like the Shwedagon Pagoda in Yangon, and some are so small and remote they don't even have a name. When you consider how religious most Myanmar people are, it's no surprise that they take great care of them. In most places, the local pagoda is obviously the pride of the town. Although the available resources of rural communities are often minimal, no expense or effort is spared to keep the pagoda in as fine a condition as possible. It doesn't matter where in Myanmar you travel, if you engage with the locals, everyone is going to encourage you to visit the local religious sites. After all, that's what many devout Buddhists in Myanmar do themselves. Pagodas are exceedingly popular pilgrimage sites, and some of the more well-known ones, such as the Myaw Yit Pagoda in the Dawei area, receive busloads of local visitors each day.

A hotel manager in Mawlamyine, the capital of Mo state once warned me: "If you don't like pagodas, there is nothing to do in Myanmar." Admittedly, although that is an exaggeration, there is some truth to his words. If you are after classical sightseeing, you will quickly realize that most of the top attractions are in fact pagodas.

One thing many pagodas have in common is that they can be found in scenic locations. The Kyaikkhami Pagoda in Mon-State was built on a rocky beach and is surrounded by glistening waters during high tide. The Su Taun Pyi Pagoda in Myitkyina is constructed on the bank of the Ayeyarwaddy and allows for some spectacular views over the flowing river. These pagodas are quite easily accessible, as they are within walking distance of nearby parking facilities and roads. However, Myanmar is not all coastline and flatlands. There are plenty of hills and mountains too, and as you might have noticed, many of them are home to little, golden pagodas. They look beautiful from a distance, and if they are well lit, they can almost look like twinkling stars at night.

Some of the more prestigious hilltop pagodas rank highly on some tourists' to-do lists. The Kyaiktiyo Pagoda on the Golden Rock in Mon-State is not just a main pilgrimage site, but it is also touted as a key highlight by every single guidebook that was ever written about Myanmar. In Mandalay, most visitors plan on working their way up Mandalay Hill just to make it to the terraces of the Sutaungpyei Pagoda. And this climb is exactly what this chapter is about.

As attractive as a pagoda on a hill might look, climbing them is where it can quickly become complicated. For the most part, Myanmar is a hot country: daytime temperatures rarely drop below 30°C. However, the plains of central Myanmar are renowned for being particularly troublesome. Throughout April, the average daytime high in Mandalay is an insane 38.9°C. At these temperatures, most western travelers cannot spend five minutes outside an air-conditioned room without sweating profusely, much less climb a hill.
On my first trip to Myanmar, I hired a guide for a day trip around Mandalay on a motorbike. Our first stop in the morning was - you guessed it - Mandalay Hill. He

was smart enough to head there first thing in the morning to take advantage of the slightly cooler temperature. My guide dropped me off at one of the stairways without ticket controls, which seemed like a good idea to me. Who doesn't want to save a few dollars here and there?

I was surprised he didn't follow me up the hill, but he said that he had previously suffered from tuberculosis and as a result, he couldn't climb stairs anymore. Thinking back, I am not sure if what he said was actually true, or if he'd just used it as an excuse. I couldn't hold it against him if he just made it up. I am pretty sure that none of the Mandalay guides are enough of a masochist to regularly follow their customers up Mandalay Hill. Regardless of that, I went on my way.

Two enormous, grand lions guard the main gate to Mandalay Hill; it's here where your climb is likely to start. You must be well prepared, as you'll need to conquer around 230m of altitude and climb 1,729 steps to reach the top of Mandalay Hill. The blistering heat is guaranteed to make it feel a lot more arduous than that. Trust me, each flight of stairs is going to make you feel increasingly miserable. Unless you are super fit and used to the heat, it can be a hellish experience.

Take my advice: persist. Once you're halfway up, you don't want to turn back, knowing that the effort was all in vain. In Myanmar, people consider the climb to a pagoda a meritorious deed, so at least you are going to do something good for your karma. If you happen to be interested in finding out just how productive your sweat glands are, this is the most effective way. Let me just tell you, it is a lot more than you may think. Around halfway up, you are going to be so soaked in sweat it wouldn't make a difference if you jumped straight into the moat around Mandalay Palace. The more you overheat on the way up the hill, the more enticing this idea will become to you, regardless of how murky the waters of the Palace may be. The only saving grace is that there is a roof over the stairways, so at least there is plenty of shade as you climb. There are often also benches to sit down on between each flight of stairs to gather your breath.

After a few more meters of pure agony, you will come across the road that connects the summit to the city. Here is where you are going to realize that battling your way up the grueling staircase was not the necessary evil that you thought it was. This might become a handy tip later on: there is another way to enjoy the view from the top.

Yes, while you are pushing yourself close to a heat stroke, most people just take a car or a motorbike to get up Mandalay Hill. It's too bad your guide forgot to mention that. Or maybe you are just one of these people who dislike doing things the easy way, and want the "authentic" experience? In my case, I simply didn't know that there was a road going up the hill - my guide didn't mention it. It turned out that when my guide said he was going to drop me off at a gate without a ticket counter, what he meant was that by not taking the road up the hill we don't have to pass the gate that makes sure all foreigners have a valid ticket. On the positive side, burning through some calories is sometimes just what you need after a hearty breakfast in one of the numerous teashops.

If seeing tourists being driven up the hill in an air-conditioned car isn't enough to kill what's left of your motivation to continue, Mandalay Hill has another surprise in store for you. On the way up you are going to pass two golden stupas with a viewing terrace around them, the so-called Shweyattaw and Byar Deik Paye Buddha images. Every time you get to the Buddha images, you'll naively think for a moment that you have made it to the top of Mandalay Hill, just to quickly realize they are a mere pitstop and you have a long way left to go. It's almost like they were built only to tease you. Just another one of these *"Only in Myanmar!"* moments. The positive side of it is that by pretending to study them, you can get some more rest without appearing like the lazy, out of shape bum that you are.

As with everything in Myanmar, it takes time to reach your destination. If your fitness level is anything like mine, you will spend half your time resting on one of the benches along the way, trying to catch your breath and avoid the looming heat exhaustion. But, given your iron will, you will eventually get there. While you climb the last few stairs trying not to collapse, the tourists you previously saw breezing up the hill in a car will use an escalator to get from the car park to the summit. It's outrageous. You had to push yourself to the limits to make it, and all they had to do is sit in a car, and then stand on an escalator.

In the end, the Sutaungpyei Pagoda will sparkle the same for the both of you. On top of that, they will enjoy the same majestic view over Mandalay that you fought your way up here for. It's okay to be slightly irritated about that. And yes, Herr Schmidt will look at you with a confused face and mutter to his wife: "Sieglinde! Look at zee crasy Mann. He valked up zee moundain." Thank god, "Ja, Ja Heinrich," is all the not-so spry retiree is going to be able to respond. After all, when you are too busy fidgeting around with your lavish hand fan and complaining about "ze heat", you don't have much time to notice what's going on around you. Don't fret, after you catch your breath, you can enjoy your sense of superiority for being a hardcore traveler who experiences the country as you were supposed to, and for not being one of these fair-weather package tourists. So even though the view might be the same you still get your special sense of reward.

So, is the view worth it? Does it make up for the agony of the climb? I will let you be the judge on that. One thing is for sure, Mandalay looks so damn good from up here. The palace with the walls and the moats around it are a powerful reminder that this was once the home of Thibaw Min, Myanmar's last king. After Myanmar's defeat in the Third Anglo-Burmese War in 1885, British forces reached Mandalay and demanded the immediate surrender of the kingdom. The once-proud sovereign of the Konbaung Dynasty was forced to leave Myanmar and live in exile in Ratnagiri, India until his death in 1916. The fantastic book called "The Glass Palace" by Amitav Ghosh is an excellent read before you come to Myanmar. It covers a wealth of interesting historical aspects of the time of Thibaw Min's dethronement and gives you a much deeper appreciation of Mandalay's history.

It's worth checking out some of the art that is made here when you are on the way back down from the summit. If you can haggle a little, you can find some good bargains. A painting from Myanmar can be an excellent souvenir for your home. As I sit here writing this book, I can see two small, black and white paintings on the walls of my apartment, brought here from Mandalay Hill. They are commonly sold all over the stairways and only cost a few Kyats.

Trying to avoid becoming completely exhausted when walking along the stairways will also make it much easier to focus on what is going on around you. Watching people go about their everyday life is very interesting anywhere in Myanmar, but on Mandalay Hill, it's even better. It doesn't matter if it's the artists, monks, vendors, pilgrims or the lay people who take care of the pagodas and stairways. Despite the high tourist numbers, this portion of the hill has retained a beautiful atmosphere. As usual, most of the tourists follow the "beaten track". For Mandalay Hill, that means taking a bus or a taxi to the top and walking the last flights of stairs or using the elevator. Many of the other stairways in the lower and middle sections of the hill are by no means crowded or busy. If you take your time, you will feel the holiness and serenity that is omitted by nature and the religious architecture. The hill is an oasis of peace within busy Mandalay. What a contrast to the chaotic roads where danger is only one wrong step away at all times.

A lot of the hill pagodas in Myanmar offer an easier alternative to get to the top. In Mawlamyine's Kyeik Than Lan Pagoda you can you use an elevator, and in Yangon's Shwedagon Pagoda you can use an escalator. If you're feeling particularly lazy you can even have someone carry you all the way up to the Kyaiktiyo Pagoda (Golden Rock) on a litter. I adore all the crazy traditions and customs of Myanmar, but this is a bit too much for me. No one should be carried around on a litter just because they are too lazy to walk. The pictures of tourists on litters being carried up the hill remind me of the darkest ages of colonial rule in Africa and Asia. Just take a motorized vehicle if you can't walk up to the Golden Rock on your own.

The question you might ask yourself now is if it's worth it to walk or not. This is something you need to decide for yourself. There is, of course, nothing wrong with taking the easy route if you don't feel fit enough to walk and still want to see the pagodas. But if you can walk, I strongly advise you to do so. The pain you need to get through is going to make the whole experience much more memorable and will give you a strong sense of accomplishment for making it to the top.

No way would I have been able to recollect my visit to Mandalay Hill in 2010 in this book if I didn't have to go up those punishing stairways. Walking also means spending more time at the site, of course. This will be time you need to understand and absorb the holy atmosphere of a pilgrimage site. Just driving up to a pagoda, walking around for 10 minutes and then leaving might be comfortable but it won't leave as lasting an impression on you.

As with any religious site in Myanmar, it's essential to be respectful. Although it's hot, women should cover their shoulders and wear trousers or a long skirt. Despite what some guidebooks say, it is generally acceptable for men to wear shorts. Just make sure the clothes you wear don't look too unkempt. Make sure you drink enough water to compensate for all the sweating you will go through on your way up. Avoid using your hands or feet to point at anything. Women are not allowed to touch monks. Pay attention to where people take off their shoes, so you don't accidentally forget to take off your shoes in a holy area. This happens quite frequently because there are often no visible signs informing you of where you can and where you can't wear footgear. And one last piece of advice, try not to ignore the warning signs of a heat stroke. You don't want to ruin your

holiday by visiting one of Myanmar's not so comfy
hospitals.

7. The Teachings of the Sayadaws

To many in the west, it came as a shock when they read the cover story of the July edition of the famous Time magazine in 2013. A picture of Ashin Wirathu and the headline "The face of Buddhist terror" was enough to shatter the global reputation of Buddhism, a religion many believed to be more peaceful and moral than all other world religions. For the first time ever, Myanmar`s religious tensions became a topic of interest in Europe and America. These problems couldn't have come at a worse time. After all the years of isolation and military dictatorship, it seemed like Myanmar had finally caught a break. The good news about the country's transition to democracy had dominated the news coverage and improved the country's international reputation. It's lamentable that the religious conflicts ended this brief spell all too fast.

Following the Time magazine's article, Myanmar's clergy (called Sangha in Buddhism) had come under sharp criticism. Journalists, especially the ones from Western countries, started researching the details, hoping to find out what was going on. Many people couldn't believe how the once-celebrated monks of Myanmar turned to hatred and ignorance in such a short period of time. It truly was a bizarre turn of events. Myanmar`s monks were an international symbol for the decade long fight for justice and resistance against Myanmar's military dictatorship. So much so that the protests of August, September and October 2007 were deemed the "Saffron Revolution". The term saffron was used because of the color of the robes worn by monks in Theravada Buddhism. Only six years after being oppressed by the military dictatorship, it seemed like it was the monks themselves who had become the oppressor.

Of course, in reality, things aren't that easy. Media outlets are keen on selling their stories, which unfortunately tend to be very one-sided when it comes to Myanmar. Were the monks of the Saffron Revolution the same ones that looted Muslim villages in Rakhine State? Is it really Buddhism that promotes hatred or is it maybe the previously ruling junta that controls a part of the clergy? All of this makes for a very complicated topic because even though the monks might appear to be a uniform entity, they are very much divided into different groups.

It's unclear where the line between religion and politics needs to be drawn in modern-day Myanmar. Wirathu and many other monks of the Ma Ba Tha (or Patriotic Association of Myanmar in English) are directly supporting the USDP, a party that consists of ex-military personnel that used to be close to the infamous junta. They also consistently highlight the vital role Myanmar's military (called Tatmadaw) plays for the future of the country. In my opinion, Myanmar's Bin Laden, as the Time magazine called Wirathu, is first and foremost a politician that uses the respect and immunity given to him by wearing a saffron robe to follow his political agenda. It's very unfortunate that the holiness and honor that is associated with monkhood gets tarnished in such a way. This is a prime example of how unscrupulous the military is in its pursuit of power and influence.

Although most news reports about Myanmar have painted a disastrous picture in recent years, it would be wrong to think of Myanmar people as a group of radical nationalists that have forgotten everything the Buddha ever taught. I find it very unfortunate that the media outlets tend to focus on the sensationalist stories that generate a lot of revenue, instead of trying to paint a fair picture of what is going on. Myanmar is no exception to this fact. There is no denying how adverse the impact of Wirathu and the monks of "Ma Ba Tha" has been. In the chapter about the beaches of southern Myanmar, you will find a first-hand account of how my family has experienced a significant abuse of our legal rights due to these nationalistic monks. Yet, I do not hold a grudge against Myanmar's Sangha. It's important to realize that extremists like Wirathu do not represent Myanmar's clergy as a whole. Forgetting about all the great monks of Myanmar just because of these extremists would be a shame and doesn't do the country justice.

In recent months a lot of good news surfaced, but admittedly, you will have to look a bit closer. I am afraid the good news doesn't sell as well as the horror stories. They just don't make it on the covers of prominent magazines and newspapers. In 2017, Myanmar's highest Buddhist authority, the "State Sangha Maha Nayaka Committee", has disbanded Ma Ba Tha on the grounds of the group not having been formed according to Sangha regulations. Furthermore, in May 2019, the government issued an arrest warrant against Wirathu. The arrest warrant is based on Wirathu allegedly spreading hatred against Aung San Suu Kyi, and the government in general.

Hopefully, the days of Wirathu spreading hatred are over. I am quite optimistic that Myanmar's monks are on their way to resolve the religious problems and once again become a symbol of human value and righteousness. Myanmar, and the world in general, would be a better place if people paid more attention to listening to what the Buddha taught.

Even though Myanmar's reputation is tarnished for now, the immensely valuable contributions Myanmar monks have made to Theravada Buddhism over the last century remain. I highly recommend reading one or two books of the well-known Sayadaws (an honorary title for a great monk). You don't have to be particularly interested in Buddhism or religion in general, to find them enjoyable.

The books I recommend are Sayadaw U Pandita's book "On the Way to Freedom" and Sayadaw U Jotika's "Snow in the Summer". Both are excellent books and absolute classics amongst western Buddhists. It doesn't matter what religion you follow or if you aren't religious at all, these books will help you to understand how our minds work. They contain valuable universal truths that can help you to live your life more peacefully. That's the beauty of Buddhist teachings, they are all about making our own lives less stressful and reduce our suffering. You don't have to believe in anything. You don't have to follow dogmas. Everything written in these books can be verified by just looking into your own mind.

I admit, reading these books doesn't have much to do with travelling in Myanmar itself. You can read them from the comforts of your own home, and the things they teach apply universally - they aren't limited to life in Myanmar. Still, I consider it a very worthwhile experience to read them. Understanding how valuable the teachings of the Myanmar Sayadaws are, gives you a more significant appreciation for the religious aspects of life in Myanmar. Buddhism really is an integral part of the country's culture, and considering most people visit Myanmar predominantly because they are curious about the culture, it can only make your visit more pleasurable to understand a thing or two about Buddhism. Without any appreciation and understanding of Buddhism, many of Myanmar's most famous sights will not reveal their real magic to you. Considering that pagodas are often the main attractions, learning some of the basics of Buddhism before your arrival is probably going to help you more than putting hours into studying every page of your Myanmar guidebook. Don't miss your chance to get the most out of your Myanmar travels just because you didn't know anything about Buddhism.

8. Myanmar: The World's Friendliest People

Myanmar offers an incredible wealth of attractions to its visitors: colonial architecture, ancient pagodas, untouched beaches, snow-capped Himalayan mountains, the mighty Ayeyarwaddy River - the list seems endless. There is no doubt that you would need several months to fully experience all the marvels of this expansive country. I admit Myanmar isn't the only country in the world that offers a variety of natural wonders, combined with a plethora of cultural sites. However, there is one thing that makes Myanmar stand out from the rest of the world. The one deciding aspect that converts so many first-time visitors into Myanmar regulars. And that's the deeply diverse people that are proud to call these lands their home.

When you read what people write about their trips to Myanmar, you will quickly realize how correct I am. The unbelievable number of ancient pagodas in Bagan might impress them, yes. After all, they are so much less crowded than the comparable ruins of Angkor Wat in Cambodia. The beauty of Inle Lake with its floating villages, tribal cultures and fishermen is genuinely enchanting for many, of course. However, take a moment and pay attention to what people really get emotional about, and you will realize that the *people* are the number one attraction in Myanmar.

I can't count how many times I've heard the people in the seats next to me on my outbound flight rave about how Myanmar is the actual "Land of Smiles", and not Thailand. They'll rejoice about how the people were so lovely and welcoming, and even invited them into their own family homes and fed them a great feast. They'll regale their friends with accounts of how nobody tried to rip them off, and quite often would even refuse to take money for services. Sometimes even crazy stories will arise, like how locals helped them out when they got lost in the middle of nowhere and lent them their motorbike for an hour so they could get back to their guesthouse.

As with many other aspects of life in Myanmar, it's hard to grasp how this is possible. How can a country that was characterized by decades of dictatorship, indoctrination, poverty and isolation be inhabited by people that welcome every visitor as if he was their long-lost child? How can they be so hospitable and generous when they often don't even have enough for themselves? And how is it possible, that despite the difficult situation they are living in, they have still retained the ability to offer you the most genuine and heartfelt smiles you will ever receive? How can there be such a wide contrast between what characterizes the shady political elites, and the ordinary people you see on your travels? Are they simply that different, or is there something else that we might overlook?

There are a few stories I could tell you about friendliness in Myanmar. One of the best ones is probably an experience I had on my first journey, way back in 2010.

I visited Pyin U Lwin and wanted to head deeper into the highlands of Shan-State. I think it was Hsipaw that I planned to travel to. One of the easiest ways to get around Myanmar is via a shared taxi. I had my guesthouse book a seat on one for the trip, and as it turned out, shared taxis are a great way to make friends. I couldn't have predicted how awesome this journey was going to be, and it all started when that taxi picked me up from my guesthouse in the early morning hours.

I was the first passenger of the day and as a consequence, I spent the first hour waiting for the taxi to pick up all the other passengers. It turned out they were spread all over Pyin U Lwin, and if that wasn't bad enough, the driver often had issues finding the right houses. It was quite a dull start to the day to say the least. However, showing patience before we could finally start our journey east was well worth it.

As usual in Myanmar, two people had to share the passenger seat in the front, and another three were placed next to me in the back. Needless to say, the car we were travelling in was a (t)rusty old Corolla.

As it turned out, the Chinese-Myanmar woman next to me was working in Taiwan and had travelled to Myanmar to visit her family and friends. She must have been around 45 to 50 years old and spoke quite decent English. She asked me where I was going and was surprised that I was actually in this part of the country. Most people in Myanmar are generally surprised to see travelers outside the main tourist centers of Yangon, Mandalay, Bagan and Inle Lake. After a while, she convinced me to follow her to Lashio, so she and her family could show me the town and its surroundings.

It sounded like a great idea to me. I didn't have many plans for my visit to Hsipaw, so I agreed to change my travel plan to Lashio instead. This kind of thing might be considered unorthodox in some countries, but this truly is a fantastic example of the friendliness of the people in Myanmar.

Most of the roads through the lowlands of central Myanmar bore me. Everything is so flat, and the lack of vegetation makes for meagre viewing. Commonly, through the last months before the arrival of the rainy season, everything around Mandalay turns into a brown semi-desert. The drive through the Shan highlands was much more enjoyable; all the hills ensure there are plenty of winding roads complete with beautiful views. The Shan highlands are also much more forested, and due to the cooler climate are home to many types of flowers, and fields of crops (such as strawberries or grapes) that can't be harvested in other parts of the Golden Country. Lashio is the biggest town in the northern part of Shan-State and isn't far from the Chinese border. I think it took around eight hours to make it to Lashio from Pyin U Lwin – quite a journey.

Once we arrived in Lashio we went to have dinner at a restaurant, and then my host family dropped me off at the state-run Lashio Motel. I guess it was the only place they knew of that could accommodate foreign travelers in this city. I didn't know how to feel about that because back in 2010 there was a big debate ongoing amongst western tourists and travel journalists, as to whether or not it was considered moral to travel to Myanmar. The idea behind it was that every foreign tourist brings the junta foreign dividends which would extend its grip on power. To reduce the income the junta earned from tourists, everyone was urged not to use the state-run hotels and travel services - like Myanma Airways, trains and museums. And there I was, in a state-run hotel, handing over my US dollars.

Thank God the generals allowed the transformation to a democracy, despite the $15 they got from me. On a more serious note, I am pretty sure the international community and their sanctions didn't do anything but make life harder for the regular people in Myanmar. It wasn't a lack of funds that made the military transform the country. How would they ever run out of money when they could export jade, gold, rubies, gas and oil to their neighbors?

I still remember the breakfast I was served on the following morning in the hotel. A member of the staff guided me to my table, which was located in a grand hall that looked as though it was used for the reception of high-ranking government officials in Lashio. Many Myanmar flags and banners with government "information" decorated the ceilings, walls and stage of this building. I felt like I was on the set of a movie that depicted life the Soviet Union in the 1980s. Just like the rest of this establishment, the breakfast hall felt depressing and awkwardly out of touch with the rest of the country.

Sadly, the standout thing that made this breakfast memorable was simply how terrible it was. All the other hotel guests were Myanmar nationals and got served a serving of fried rice, whereas fried eggs and toast was all they had in mind for me. There is little that you can do wrong when frying an egg and placing it on a slice of toast, right? Wrong. The "fried" egg I received looked like it saw the pan for a total of 10 seconds and was nowhere near done when it landed on my plate. The toast was everything but fresh, and the margarine on it tasted like a weapon of chemical warfare. It tasted so awful I couldn't even force myself to eat more than a tiny piece.

I guess they bought the toast and margarine months ago, so just in case a foreigner shows up they have something to serve him. As everyone knows, us westerners can't eat anything more than horrible margarine and toast for breakfast.

Fortunately, this story isn't just about breakfast but rather about what happened next; my gracious host family picked me up in a rugged pickup truck, and we embarked on a delightful tour around Lashio.

I was seated in the open-top cargo bed with a guy that must have been a younger brother or some other relative of the women I'd met in the taxi. It was in fact quite a hilarious situation. In 2010, foreign visitors were an extremely rare sight in Lashio, and everyone in the streets was staring at us. Strangely, he absolutely reveled in the attention. He would wave and shout something towards everyone gazing in our direction. I guess he felt like a king parading around town on this day.

One of the first stops we made was at the Yan Tine Aung pagoda, located right at the highway on the western fringes of the city. This is perhaps Lashio's most memorable site owing to the scenic views across the green, rolling Shan hills. There are also hot water springs in Lashio, which serve as a widely popular destination for some of the day-tripping locals of the area. The pools don't look very welcoming, but that doesn't stop anyone from enjoying the thermal water. I guess this must be the perfect spot to warm up in during the cold winter mornings of the Shan highlands. I know that we visited a few more pagodas, but I don't properly remember any of them.

The only place that I do remember quite clearly was the small sewing factory. If I remember right, a member of the family actually worked there, and that was the reason we visited it. Around 30 women were working there, using mechanical sewing machines and working quite hard with them. Undoubtedly, the level of pay they received nowhere near matched the amount of effort they put in. The sight of a weird tourist spontaneously appearing in their factory must have added some much-needed variety to their otherwise monotonous workday.

It was amazing how much my host family did for me so that I could have an enjoyable and memorable day in their city. After all this touring we had dinner in a restaurant. I finally wanted to use this chance to give something back for all the efforts they made and attempted to cover the bill for our food. Can you guess what happened? They refused to accept my money. What better example of the fantastic hospitality of Myanmar's people? Where else would you experience this? Damn right, *Only in Myanmar!*

As impressive as experiences like the one I described in this chapter are, all the little everyday moments of kindness are often just as charming. I remember one of the guys at my local airport in Myitkyina very well. He worked for one of the domestic airlines and had the task of handling the luggage. Many of Myanmar's domestic airports don't have luggage belts, and the suitcases and bags are often put on a rolling car and transported to the exit area of the airport. Then passengers give the airport staff their luggage tag, and they bring you your bags for a small tip of 500 or 1000 Kyats. Every time he spotted me, he gave me a big smile, a pat on the shoulder and made some weird jokes. He didn't speak good English, and I usually didn't get what he meant, but it was a fun and pleasant experience regardless. It was almost like a ritual of being welcomed back to town.

People here love having a bit of fun with you. The children especially. They just love teasing foreign tourists. I had many humorous moments wherein groups of village kids would repeatedly run up to us, shout "hello" or "mingala ba", just to then run away in laughter. I am sure I must have looked like an alien to them, and they told everyone their funny story about how they saw these bizarre tourists today. This frequently happened on the lonely beaches in southern Myanmar. In fact, I am quite sure the children of the village Kampani (between Maungmakan Beach and the Myaw Yit Pagoda) have made it their favorite hobby to surprise the foreign visitors of the beach adjacent to the village. I have seen them do this to plenty of tourists during the days we spent in the village. So, don't be surprised if your tranquil beach experience gets interrupted briefly by a group of children laughing about your big nose and "yellow" (people in Myanmar aren't familiar with the color blond) hair. It's all good fun, so relax and make sure they keep on laughing.

Try asking someone for directions when wandering around the streets of a small town, and you'll notice that everyone in the surrounding area will come over to try and help. They are making finding out where you are trying to go and how to give you the right directions a real team effort. If all of this turns out to be too complicated, someone will go and get his motorbike, and before you know it, you will find yourself on the back of it, getting a free ride to what hopefully turns out to be your desired destination. I have experienced this exact scenario plenty of times on my first travels in Myanmar.

Let me tell you, if you ask for help in Myanmar you will get more than what you thought you were asking for.

Many of the locals are also incredibly curious and are always eager to have a chat; this is especially true for the older generations. If you sit down in a small establishment like a noodle stall or one of the many delicious Indian chapati or puri shops (often found next to mosques) you will often end up having an interesting conversation. Many speak decent English and will appreciate the opportunity to practice it a bit more by having a genuine conversation with you. Of course, they are also very curious about how you feel about Myanmar, what places you are planning to visit, if you are travelling alone (something that seems very strange to them) and so on. It was surprising to me that even in 2010, people openly talked about politics and weren't afraid to criticize the military in public. I found that people are less intimidated about interacting with you if you are on your own, which is good news for solo travelers. Of course, it's possible they are just worried that you'll feel lonely and bored - who knows? Often you will notice that someone wants to say something to you but is hesitant about it; just say a few words to break the ice.

Another great consequence of meeting people is that often they will even invite you to their homes for lunch or dinner. Don't turn down the chance of visiting a Myanmar family, if you are genuinely interested in finding out how the regular people live in this country. Even if most people's houses are very humble, compared to their counterparts in western countries, they will proudly show you around. You can be sure that the whole family is going to come around for this special occasion and you will be introduced to everyone. You'd better have a strong memory for names! The women of the families will try their absolute best to serve up a feast of traditional Myanmar food to spoil you with. No expense will be spared to cook up heaps of delicious food. Visiting a family in their home is one of the most unforgettable experiences you will have on your travels. Not only that, but by getting such an authentic and personal insight, you will learn more about Myanmar than any sightseeing trip could ever teach you.

Of course, even the many family-run guesthouses can be an excellent way to experience the beautiful ways in which the locals make you feel welcome. I have spent many hours watching TV, playing cards or just chatting with the families and staff of the guesthouses I've stayed in. Many places will make you feel like you are much more than only a paying customer. You feel genuinely welcome, one more experience that is uniquely Myanmar and hard to find elsewhere.

At some point during your trip you might come back to the question of how it is possible that there seems to be such a big contrast between the sweetness of regular Myanmar people and the way the country was run for decades. If you have been to neighboring countries like Thailand and India, you might also wonder why it is that the people here are so kind to you when elsewhere all that seemed to be of interest was where your tourist dollars went. For people who are genuinely interested in the country, it's certainly interesting to reflect on these things.

My opinion is that the friendliness you encounter in Myanmar is partly due to the hierarchical way the society works. You are considered rich for being able to travel in Myanmar, and because of that you automatically place high in the society. Unfortunately, the respect you experience isn't the way people generally treat each other in Myanmar. This hierarchical thinking is probably one of the main reasons the political elites have ignored the interests of those below them for such a long time.

Another big aspect is that western tourists were a rare sight in virtually any place that wasn't on the primary tourist circuit (Yangon, Mandalay, Bagan, Inle Lake). That means you are interesting just because you stand out so much. Of course, short term commercial interests also matter. If a taxi driver is approaching you with a big smile, he probably isn't after friendship, so much as a new customer. The fact that tourists are such a rare sight in Myanmar means that most locals have never had any negative experiences with them. I am sure this aspect also plays a significant role in their friendliness and hospitality. Unfortunately, it's all too easy to build up stereotypes about a particular group of people just because of a few bad experiences you may have had.

Due to these factors, it remains to be seen if the higher tourist arrival numbers change the attitude of the local population as they did in mainstream tourist destinations like Thailand, where the slogan "Land of Smiles" has long been nothing but a smart marketing strategy. Please keep in mind that it's up to every one of us to maintain the, for now, excellent reputation tourists in Myanmar enjoy. Act respectful and show your thankfulness for how warmly you were welcomed into their towns and villages.

9. The Betel Nut.

Myanmar is a country full of wonders, waiting to be explored. It doesn't matter how you travel, by the end of your trip you will have seen, and experienced unique things not found anywhere else in the world. This is the same whether you're taking a luxurious Ayeyarwaddy cruise or backpacking through scruffy guesthouses. If you're travelling through Yangon or Bagan or trekking through a remote village of the Chin mountains. It's guaranteed: once you arrive back at Yangon International Airport to board your return flight to the 'normal world', you'll realize just how special Myanmar is.

You'll discover things that were new to you and that you haven't come across in any other country before arriving in Myanmar. There will be intense encounters that broaden your mental horizon and impact your view of the world. Some of these experiences will have been nice, such as the unparalleled friendliness and hospitality that you encounter everywhere, but there will also be unpleasant moments, like when you are increasingly worried you will not make it to catch your flight because you are stuck in one of Yangon's monstrous traffic jams. Finally, there are the moments that just confuse you, moments that you can't comprehend because you have no clue what actually happened.

Myanmar is one of these countries that make visitors do some additional research prior arrival. Is it safe? What's the deal with having to carry crisp US dollar bills? Are there really no ATMs anywhere? Where do I get a sim-card for my phone? I had all these things covered when I boarded the plane to Yangon in summer 2010, but there was one little thing I'd overlooked, and good old Myanmar taught me a lesson right after my arrival. I used a taxi to get to my hotel in downtown Yangon. Yes, it was one of the old rusty Corollas, but that wasn't much of a surprise; I had seen pictures of these vans in my guidebook before my arrival. We had a red light at the first major intersection after the airport, and this is where it all began, another one of these unique *"Only in Myanmar"* moments. My taxi driver stopped the car, opened his door and spat a mouthful of some mysterious, red liquid on the road. I didn't know what the hell he was doing. I was perplexed and wondered if maybe it wasn't such a good idea to come here. The thing that scared me was that he was profoundly coughing. Was it actually blood? Was there some unseen danger here?

Firstly, tuberculosis came to mind, or maybe some other infectious disease? Looking back at this experience makes me laugh. I was very naive and way too scared. Myanmar has a way of making travelers paranoid and worried, just to then prove them wrong. I guess that is what happens when you are incredibly paranoid from hearing so many bad things about the place you are visiting, and then, in reality, realize that you are perfectly safe, and there is a reasonable explanation behind all the worries and doubts that might arise. No, I didn't catch tuberculosis and no, the taxi guy wasn't ill either. All he did was chew on some betel nut. Amongst taxi drivers in Myanmar, this is entirely normal and the best way of making the day a little bit easier to get through. That happened in 2010 and granted the country has changed a lot since then. Some of the unique aspects of travelling here might be disappearing as Myanmar becomes more modern. However, I can promise you, the habit of chewing betel nut hasn't changed all that much.

What is known as betel nut is actually areca nut, with slaked lime and catechu wrapped up in a green betel leaf. Some vendors also mix in tobacco and spices like chili. Myanmar people call it "kunya", and many consume it daily. The red strains that the betel nut juice creates on Yangon's pavements attest to this fact. Some of the rubbish bins you see in public places, such as train stations, are often overflowing with the juices of the spat out betel nuts — not a very aesthetically pleasing sight.

Kunya has a stimulating effect that makes you feel alert and slightly euphoric, betel nut is especially popular amongst people who work hard, physically demanding jobs. Kunya is also popular amongst the countless bus and lorry drivers that navigate through Myanmar's often chaotic streets. They appreciate it for its effect to keep you awake and delay the inevitable need for sleep. The overland routes in Myanmar are usually time-consuming and challenging; it's no surprise that people resort to Kunya to get them through.

Even though betel nut is also consumed in many other countries in South-East Asia, it's definitely more prominent in Myanmar, making it a part of the unique experience of travelling in this crazy country. Charming street stands selling betel nut can be found at every corner in the villages and towns all over the numerous divisions and states that constitute modern-day Myanmar. From Myeik in the south to Myitkyina in the north, Kunya is everywhere. If you don't want to try it for yourself, taking a look at one of these small shops is still an experience in and of itself. It's fascinating to watch how the skilled vendors wrap up the leaves in record speed with a well-practiced routine and to see how popular the little bundles of betel nuts are. Many customers buy a package of three betel nuts, which only costs around 100 Kyats. Many drivers don't even get out of the car to get their betel nut fix. They simply stop their car and shout their order through the opened window. I guess that is what you call efficiency made in Myanmar.

Chewing betel nut seems like an exciting habit to us, but it's quite sad how much damage it does to the population. Due to lack of better knowledge and education, many people in Myanmar wrongly assume chewing betel nut is no big deal. In reality, it's not harmless whatsoever and poses some severe long-term health risks like oral cancer, teeth discoloration and gum damage. Even a few hours in Myanmar are enough to realize how real this problem is. It can be quite unsettling for western travelers to see in which condition the teeth and gums of long-term betel nut users are.

More relevant for you as a potential first-time user is that chewing betel nut can also cause headaches, an upset stomach and dizziness. Please keep that in mind and decide for yourself if trying it out is really worth it for you. I will be honest with you, despite living in Myanmar for a while, I've never tried it out. I was curious about "Kunya" on my first visits to Myanmar, and I once came close to sampling it when the staff of a guesthouse offered me a fresh betel nut. My wife was very adamant with her advice: she wouldn't let me try it out. I wasn't surprised in the slightest because she has the same resolute mindset about alcohol and cigarettes. She works as a teacher: do I need to say any more?

There are some efforts by the government and NGOs to increase awareness of the risks of betel nut. And indeed, the consumption amongst the younger generations is fortunately declining. However, the main reason for this is not the concern about health risks but a changing mindset of the young man in Myanmar. They didn't care too much about their appearance in the past, but with all the influences from music and soap operas, everyone wants to look like a Korean actor now. Red gums and rotten teeth just do not match with the latest clothes and hairstyles from Korea. I wish people were smart enough to turn away from Kunya because they didn't want to suffer from oral cancer, but I guess if having to listen to terrible K-Pop blasted on cheap speakers is the sacrifice it takes to reduce betel nut consumption, it's worth it in the end.

10. The Remains of British Colonialism

It is a sad story. Just after gaining independence from the British empire at the end of the Second World War, Myanmar seemed to have a promising future. National elections were held, the minorities of Myanmar signed the Paunglong contract (agreeing to become part of a federal union), and modern-day Myanmar was born. But things took a turn for the worse. After the national hero Aung San was assassinated in 1947, the country stumbled from one crisis to another, and all hope for stability and development was lost. In 1962, brutal dictator Ne Win came into power and led the country into an abyss. While the rest of the world modernized and went through sweeping changes, Myanmar was left behind. The self-imposed isolation of what was then called Burma and the lack of economic development paralyzed the country for decades. Time stood still during this era. Considering all of this, it is no surprise that Myanmar is now one of the countries with the liveliest colonial heritage.

I admit, the Brits weren't able to leave any culinary influences behind when they packed up and left after the Second World War, but there is still plenty to be experienced. Considering the state in which British cuisine has been in the past, the missing culinary footprint of British food in Myanmar might be for the best of all of us. One thing I do lament however, is the absence of a Burmese equivalent to the delicious French-inspired Banh Mi baguette sandwiches (or Num Pang in Cambodian). They are extremely popular in French

Indochina, and street vendors sell them all over Vietnam, Cambodia and Laos.

The more you understand and get to know Myanmar, the more you will realize how big of an impact the British legacy still has in the country. It only takes a few hours in Yangon to recognize that there is still plenty of colonial architecture left, but that's just scratching the surface. The railway network in Myanmar was established by the British and still plays a crucial role in the more remote areas, such as Kachin state. It's equally essential for the transport of goods and the transport of people. In the past, the railway was often the defining factor in how much of a grip Myanmar's central government could hold over ethnic regions. One thing that might surprise you on your first journey to Myanmar is the presence of many large Indian communities all over the country. The large number of Hindu temples and Muslim mosques that can be found in Myanmar's cities are a testimony to that fact. Most Myanmar-Indians are descendants of migrants who moved here when Myanmar was a province of British India. Back then, they played a leading role in the colonial administration and economy. Myanmar's diversity is, at least partially, also a result of the colonial times.

If you happen to travel in the minority areas like Kachin state, Chin state or Kayin state, you will notice many small, humble churches. They were built by British missionaries many decades ago, and even though the British left a long time ago, the work of the missionaries persists. Christianity is alive and going strong amongst many communities in the frontier areas. The British rule also had an impact on how Myanmar people like to spend their free time. Golf is one of the favorite free-time activities for the more affluent members of

Myanmar society, and, perhaps most importantly for you, the level of English proficiency is relatively high in Myanmar when compared to most South-East Asian countries. This is a significant improvement over Thailand or Vietnam, where most regular people outside the tourism industry don't speak even basic English. You will always find someone willing to help you out with a bit of English in Myanmar, and despite the country's complicated past, even the older generations often have some grasp of the English language.

The most striking examples of the remaining colonial influence can be found in Myanmar's judicial system. Many of the laws that are in effect today date back to the colonial era, and even the way the parliament is arranged is deeply inspired by the British: just like in the UK, it is split into a lower house and an upper house.

Even though you will encounter remnants of the colonial era wherever you go, some places are uniquely suited to get an idea of how Myanmar looked under British rule. One such place is charming Pyin U Lwin. It's located 90 minutes east of Mandalay and is the first town you reach after climbing the winding road up the Shan highlands. I have good news for you: if you struggle with the heat of the central plains, Pyin U Lwin is situated at an altitude of roughly 1000m. The temperatures here are much easier to handle. The cooler environment is also the reason Pyin U Lwin has so much colonial flair. To escape the grueling heat, the British administration moved to Pyin U Lwin each summer and made the town the summer capital of British Burma.

Pyin U Lwin was also the headquarters of the so-called "Burma Division", a formation mainly made up of Indians and Gorkhas. During colonial times the town was called Maymyo. Myo is the Myanmar term for city or town, and May referred to Colonel May, a veteran commander of the Bengal Regiment who founded a garrison town here. Pyin U Lwin was merely a village consisting of a few houses back then. Considering this, it's no surprise the Myanmar government was keen on renaming the town once the British left. Another interesting detail is that famed author George Orwell was also stationed in Pyin U Lwin.

Local businesspeople turned many of the old colonial residential buildings into hotels. What better way to start off your Pyin U Lwin experience than to check into one of them? Not many places in the world offer you the chance to sleep in the same - virtually unchanged- houses as the British did, 100 years ago. Don't worry about the price tag of these hotels, as even though they sound expensive, not all of them cater exclusively to luxury travelers. You can find a hotel with colonial flair to suit every budget. Most of the British residential buildings are situated in a quiet area between the town's center and the famous Kandawgyi Gardens. You will almost feel like you are in a totally different country here. The villas sit on spacious properties with well-maintained gardens, and the surrounding area is almost tranquil, with the traffic being minimal.

I recommend going for a walk and discovering the area on your feet. It's guaranteed to be stress-free. There is no better place for a casual walk than Pyin U Lwin when you also consider that there are plenty of large trees around. This vegetation provides an abundance of shade, and the slightly colder mountain air means you might spend some time without sweating profusely! After spending time in the lowlands of central Myanmar, this might start to seem like a novelty to you.

Once you've checked out the colonial neighborhoods, you can head over to the National Kandawgyi Botanical Gardens. Even though the place is a popular destination for day-trippers from Mandalay, it's not overly crowded once you've walked some distance from the central entrance area. This botanical garden was established by a British forest officer called Alex Roger. Apparently, it was modelled after the Kew Gardens of England, and resembles a British landscape. Even though there is not much colonial flair to be enjoyed in the gardens today, the experience is still worth it just for how different the park is to everyday life in Myanmar.

There are more than 480 species of flowers and trees to be found, and the entrance ticket also includes a visit to the Butterfly Museum, and the Fossils Museum. What stands out, however, is how neatly kept everything is. The park is arguably in a better condition than many botanical gardens found in Western Europe. Once you've passed the ticket counter, you will find yourself in the central area, with beautiful, broad views over the central lake. This area is usually packed with Myanmar people taking selfies in front of the flowerbeds, which is understandable.
I doubt there is another place in Myanmar with as many dazzling, colorful flowers. From here you can start your round tour through the park. If you want to make sure you don't miss anything, it's best to start with the rock garden and to then take the teak footpath through the swamp. After a few minutes you will arrive at the southern-most point of the gardens. From here you will need to follow one of the paths north, and you will eventually make it all the way around the lake. One thing you shouldn't miss is the viewing tower in the north-western corner of the park. It's a bit of a climb to make it

there, but the view over the botanical garden and Pyin U Lwin is impressive.

Too much time spent in the colonial neighborhoods and botanical gardens can cause acute Myanmar withdrawal symptoms. Once you are tired of all the tidiness of the Kandawgyi Gardens and are ready to jump back into the real world, you should visit the hectic center of Pyin U Lwin. Once you have arrived at the Purcell Tower, you'll know you have made it. Granted, the center of Pyin U Lwin doesn't offer much in terms of architectural beauty. It's also very hectic, because the main Mandalay-Lashio highway runs right through it, but it's still somewhat entertaining. There are plenty of colonial buildings everywhere and when walking the streets, it becomes apparent that many Myanmar-Indians are living here. You can find Indian sweet shops and restaurants on every corner, and because of all these influences, Pyin U Lwin feels more diverse, and unlike the rest of the places you will visit on your journey through Myanmar.

A café rarely is one of the biggest attractions of a major city, but the Maymyo Café is a real exception to that. You absolutely cannot visit Pyin U Lwin's center and not come here. If you are like me and love good coffee, this is the best place in all of Myanmar. They also serve great cakes, sandwiches and other snacks. The way the café is decorated and run, will make you forget that you are in Myanmar for a while. This place is a true oasis.

The Christian cemetery of Pyin U Lwin is another place that can be interesting for history buffs. It's located next to the Sacred Heart Catholic Church to the north of the center. It's not hard to find because it's almost directly next to the train tracks. According to the cemetery register of European burials, there are 303 recorded graves here, dating back to the time frame from 1895 to 1973. Unlike the well-known war cemeteries in Taukkyan and Thanbyuzayat, the Christian cemetery of Pyin U Lwin is not well maintained, so be prepared for some rough conditions. On the positive side, the place does not get a lot of visitors, so you will likely have it all to yourself.

Once you are done with your Pyin U Lwin visit, a shared taxi is the easiest way to get back to Mandalay. Pyin U Lwin is famous all over Myanmar for the locally grown strawberries, coffee, and flowers. Ask your driver to stop at one of the many roadside shops that line the highway to Mandalay. Depending on the season you can buy delicious, locally grown fruits and vegetables. If you have a sweet tooth, you can also try the year-round available home-made strawberry yoghurt, jam and wine.

Pyin U Lwin might not be the highest priority on your to-do list, especially if you have a tight schedule and skipping it on your first Myanmar trip might make sense. Luckily, not making it to the charming hill station doesn't mean you can't experience the colonial flair. You are very likely to use Yangon as your gateway to the country and spend at least two or three days there. Of course, Yangon is a modern city full of life and doesn't have the charming colonial feel of Pyin U Lwin. You won't be able to sleep in an old British residence, and there are also no romantic little horse carts driving you around in style. But what Yangon lacks in atmosphere it makes up for with an abundance of notable colonial buildings. Not only that, Yangon is the capital city with the highest selection of colonial buildings in all of South-East Asia. I know Yangon isn't technically the capital anymore since the government moved to

Naypyitaw in 2005, but that doesn't change the fact that Yangon is still very much the heart of Myanmar's culture and economy.

If you want to go sightseeing for colonial buildings, the list of possible spots is endless. If you have some time and don't mind walking, I can advise you to get a taxi from your hotel and go to Sule Pagoda. The city-building engineers of the British empire used the pagoda as the central point of Yangon. The streets of the downtown area are laid out in a grid. On top of that, they are usually numbered instead of named. This makes it easier to find your way around without getting lost. What better place to start a pleasant walking tour?

In close proximity to Sule Pagoda is the Yangon City Hall, an exciting blend of Western and Myanmar architecture. From here you can quite easily walk to the Saint Mary Cathedral, perhaps Myanmar's most famous church. In many ways, this building feels like a grand version of all the little red brick churches you might have seen in the Christian minority areas of Myanmar. Of course, the Saint Mary Cathedral is anything but humble and also much better maintained than its counterparts in the frontier areas. The Secretariat, the biggest colonial building of Yangon, is only a few minutes away. It was the seat of the British administration and tragically the place where Aung San and six cabinet ministers were assassinated in 1947.

It takes around 15 minutes to reach Strand Road from this grand building. Strand Road is not only home to the Strand Hotel, but also the Myanmar Port Authority, the Customs House and the headquarters of Myanma National Airlines. The Strand Hotel doesn't look too impressive from the outside, and if you don't know it's there, you might even accidentally walk past it and miss it altogether. When I first came to Yangon that actually happened to me. But that doesn't mean it's not by far the most prestigious hotel in the entire country. It was built in 1901 and despite many restorations, has remained true to its original architecture. In many ways, The Strand isn't just a luxury hotel. It's just as much part of Yangon's history as buildings like the Secretariat or the High Court. It's also the only hotel in Yangon that was awarded the blue plaque by the Yangon Heritage Trust.

If you want to spend some time in the hotel and aren't keen on paying for one of the expensive suites, you can visit the Strand Café for high tea each afternoon. A lot of places are called time capsules, which is often just an exaggeration, and there isn't much behind it. But trust me, if there is one place that can rightfully be called a time capsule, this is it. Having tea or coffee here will make you feel like it's 1920, and you are a distinguished British gentleman (or lady) on an adventurous journey into the orient. The atmosphere created by the vintage pictures of colonial Burma, the high ceilings, the teak windows and the polished wood floors genuinely make this place a remembrance of times long gone. And despite all that, the Strand Café doesn't feel like a museum. Just like 100 years ago, the café exists to spoil its visitors with the uniquely understated, yet luxurious elegance only the British have truly mastered. In this sense, the soul of this café is very much alive. No other place I have ever visited has given me that much nostalgia. History alive, *Only in Myanmar!*

Once you are back in the heat and bustle of downtown Yangon's streets, there is plenty more to see. A few minutes' walk down Strand Road, and you will come across the Police Commissioner's Building. This building is known for its 22 ionic columns, each of which was shipped in from England. From here you can make your way north to another truly grand building, the Yangon High Court. It was home to the British court and, until 2006, also the home of the supreme court of Myanmar. The supreme court has since then moved to the new administrative capital Naypyitaw. Arguably the most iconic feature of the High Court is the clock tower and the staunch, red-brick exterior. Once you are done admiring its beauty, you will find yourself right in front of Maha Bandula Park and only a few meters from your initial starting point, Sule Pagoda.

The easiest way to navigate downtown Yangon for this walking tour, is to use your smartphone. Just type in the names of the different buildings and follow the map. Ideally, you can download the maps on your phone using your hotel's wi-fi before you make it on your way to Sule Pagoda.

If all of this hasn't been enough to satisfy your interest in Myanmar's colonial past, you can also take a taxi and head to the Taukkyan War Cemetery. It's located 32km north of the Sule Pagoda. Keep in mind that the traffic in Yangon is often terrible, and depending on the time of the day, it can unfortunately take several hours to get there. The Taukkyan War Cemetery is the exact opposite of the Christian cemetery in Pyin U Lwin. It's perfectly maintained and is considered as one of the most highly rated war cemeteries in Asia. Around 6400 soldiers who died during the two world wars have found their final resting place here.

Whether it's the small things that are connected to the colonial rule or the grand architecture of downtown Yangon, if you keep your eyes open, you can spot the

British legacy in many aspects of everyday life in Myanmar. Despite all the recent changes, the country still feels like a real-life history book, and that's something unique, and refreshing. Now if only there were some Banh Mi around. Well, I guess we can't have it all.

11. The Classic Cars of Myanmar

One of the first things that comes to mind when you think of Cuba is its old, historic cars. What could be a more classical image of Cuba than an old Chrysler parked in front of a crumbling, colonial-era building in Havana? Checking out the classic cars is something most visitors to Cuba put high on their to-do list. Even though Myanmar offers a similar experience, few people are aware of this before arriving in the Golden Country. I guess the American cars from the 50s are considered a bigger attraction than the slightly more boring Toyotas and Mazdas from the 1960s, 70s and 80s, but hey, Japanese cars deserve some love too.

Before the early 2010s, new cars were considered a rare sight in Myanmar. The most common vehicles you could find in Yangon were the white Toyota Corollas built in the late 1970s, and early 1980s, with the vans built from 1981 to 1983 being the most common variant. Due to strict import regulations, these 30 to 40-year-old cars were worth a staggering 50,000 US-dollars in Myanmar. Since then, the import regulations have been relaxed, and new cars have flooded the country. Nowadays, there are even BMW and Mercedes-Benz dealerships in Yangon, among others. Consequently, the value of the iconic Corollas declined to the point of being almost entirely worthless. Whoever bought a Corolla just before the import changes wasted a small fortune on these cars, when the same money could have bought a modern car just weeks later. I can't think of a better example of the crazy economic conditions in good old Myanmar.

Even though cars are still highly taxed in Myanmar, they have gotten a lot more affordable for the middle-class citizens of the country. Before the car regulation changes, only the rich could afford cars; most of the vehicles driving around Yangon were either taxis or commercial vehicles. When I first arrived in 2010, there were no traffic jams in Yangon at all. This has changed drastically. Cars are now commonly used as a means of private transport. Though this progress is making the life of many local people more comfortable, it also means that Yangon's roads are now some of the most congested in all of South-East Asia. Road infrastructure is improving steadily, but it will take quite some time until it can cope with the explosion in car ownership. Always keep this in mind, and plan trips accordingly. This is especially important if you need to catch a plane, as it can take two hours just to get from downtown Yangon to the airport, due to the constant traffic jams.

As you might imagine, despite the dramatic increase in the total number of cars, the old Corollas are almost fading from existence, becoming much harder to spot. It´s no surprise everyone wants to trade them in for a more comfortable and reliable vehicle. That being said, when you flag down a taxi in Yangon, you might still end up journeying in a Corolla from the early 80s. If you do so, you shouldn't lament being out of luck for not having modern comforts like air-conditioning and intact seats. Instead, value the chance of experiencing what used to be the standard way of getting around Yangon. However, for a chance to do so, you must act fast. It's relatively certain that in the coming years, even the last of the charming Corolla dinosaurs will have disappeared too. At this point, the city will have been completely taken over by the same characterless cars that you already see roaming around the streets everywhere else in the world.

Unfortunately, the little Mazda taxis of Mandalay have already suffered this fate. They used to be a staple of Mandalay's roads, just like the white Toyotas. The Mazda B360 was commonly used in Myanmar and was initially built and sold in Japan throughout the 1960s. After being phased out within a few years, Toyota opened a plant in Myanmar and continued production for the local market in 1972. It's incredible how long they were used as a means of everyday transport. Together with the white Corollas, they are perfect examples of why travelling to Myanmar can sometimes feel like opening a time capsule. During my first visits to Mandalay, they were just as much of a sight to behold as some of the ancient pagodas. The government decided to ban the use of these old pick-up trucks in 2012, and they all disappeared within a few weeks. Fortunately for the taxi drivers of Mandalay, the government granted the owners of the blue Mazdas loans that allowed them to buy new vehicles. That way, they could continue earning a livelihood even without their trusty B360s. This political move made sense in terms of safety and efficiency, but it is still a shame that the nostalgic value of these little blue pick-ups wasn't appreciated. Even though they aren't fit for everyday transport in a modern city like Mandalay, they could still be a great way to get around town in a more relaxed and atmospheric way - something I am sure many tourists would appreciate. I am glad I had the chance to experience riding around Mandalay in an ancient blue Mazda and will always cherish the memory.

Besides the dreariness of modern transport, riding through Yangon or Mandalay with the windows open brings you much closer to what is going on around you. The noise, heat and smells are unfiltered, your view unobstructed by a tinted window. Yes, the seats of the Corollas have been patched over and over again; sometimes the rust might have eaten holes into the bodywork, allowing you a clear view of the road beneath, through the footwell of the car. Yes, the doors might not close properly, and there can be dust from driving around Yangon with open windows all day. Ultimately, there is a certain nostalgia to these little, old Corollas. If you have been in Myanmar before the transition to democracy begun, each drive in these iconic dinosaurs is going to remind you of your first time here, when everything was different and exciting, and travelling here felt even more adventurous than it does now. It's almost like how certain songs, places or moments can remind you of meeting a particular person; these little Corollas remind you of how it all started: how your love affair with this country began. Their disappearance is a symbol for the transition Myanmar is going through.

12. Feel Like Robinson Crusoe.

Many Myanmar visitors, especially the ones that arrive here for the first time, frequently overlook Southern Myanmar. This can often be considered a good thing because that means the beautiful, sprawling beaches are usually empty and completely untouched. Where else in South-East Asia can you find deserted beaches that can be reached just by renting a motorbike and going on your way? The Myeik Archipelago is the best-known travel destination in the south of Myanmar. The vast archipelago right in front of the charming city of Myeik has incredible visiting potential. However, all the beaches can only be reached by boat tours, which can unfortunately be rather expensive and are only possible with guides. Considering all these drawbacks, the best place to travel to for beautiful beach discoveries is Dawei, the administrative capital of Tanintharyi Division.

If you are travelling around Myanmar and decide to go exploring in Dawei, you have several transport options available. You can either hop on a plane from Yangon or take the train or even a bus. Needless to say, the train is the slowest, longest and least comfortable option. If you decide to take a bus, it will take roughly ten hours to get there. Unlike most other places in Myanmar, you can also make it to Dawei from Bangkok. Direct bus services that connect both cities are now available. Considering that the road conditions on the Myanmar side of the border are constantly improving, and Bangkok is for many the gateway to South-East Asia, this is a real, viable alternative. For now, it's certainly an adventure in and of itself.

Dawei is a city of around 180,000 people but isn't as hectic as you would expect. It's by far the cleanest and best-maintained city I've visited in Myanmar. The roads are in pristine condition and even have markings on them, aiding the flow of traffic. I suspect they were built in cooperation with the Thai companies that work on the Dawei Special Economic Zone and the port project north of Dawei. Unfortunately, the smooth roads can only be found in Dawei and towards the mega project in the north. On your way to the beaches, you will find yourself on regular Myanmar roads once again, with all the potholes and generally uneven surfaces you would expect.

Right in the middle of Dawei, you will find a decently stocked supermarket. It's called Ahla Thit Shopping Center and is located on the corner of Yay Road and Myotwin Road. It has everything you need at fair prices. Dawei also has a modern hospital - at least for Myanmar standards. Most importantly, there are several attractive accommodation options available, no matter what budget you're travelling on. From simple guesthouses to recently opened luxury hotels, you will find everything you need in Dawei.

As anywhere in Myanmar there are a few charming pagodas that you can visit. This might be interesting if it's your first trip to Myanmar; for more seasoned Myanmar travelers however, the Dawei pagodas probably aren't very high on their to-do lists. For me, my highlight and potentially my favorite thing to do is to eat out at night. The streets are most alive after 8pm, and everyone seems to be out to snack or have a beer.

Although most cities in Myanmar have night markets, the streets of Dawei are way livelier than anything I experienced in upper Myanmar.

Another plus is that the food in Dawei is quite different from the rest of the country. You can find some classical Myanmar restaurants and (not so great) teashops, but most establishments seem to serve an exciting fusion of Burmese and Thai food. There are also a lot of restaurants that serve wholesome, classic Thai food.

As with the hotels, there are restaurants for every budget, from basic road-side stalls to expensive eateries that cater towards foreign travelers. However, the most basic places often serve the best food. Nothing beats walking around and trying out some of the most delicious looking snacks on offer. If It's your kind of thing, cold beer with some BBQ is also a fantastic way to spend the evening. Acting as a headquarters for your beach expeditions, Dawei is genuinely perfect. I'm not sure about you, but beach hunting during the day, and snack hunting during the evening sounds like awesome fun to me.

Even though Dawei is a pleasant city, no one comes here for the town itself. If you want to visit pagodas you can just stay in Yangon or Mandalay. It's all about the beaches - exploring them on the back of a motorbike might be my absolute favorite thing to do. And I don't just mean in Myanmar: if you asked me what I'd like to do the most tomorrow, I would say ride a motorbike to a beach in Dawei. Yes, it's that fun. It's about as adventurous as travelling in Myanmar can be. The sense of freedom and exploration is near-impossible to beat.

A word of caution though: you need to be a somewhat competent motorbike rider. Although Dawei is not overly busy, there is still plenty of traffic on the main roads. To reach the beaches, you will often need to ride on dirt tracks and traverse up or down steep hills. This is not something that an inexperienced rider can safely do. If you do feel competent enough to go exploring on a bike, then please always wear a helmet, both for safety and to avoid trouble with the police. Rental motorbikes can be found in Dawei and also at the guesthouses and hotels in Maungmakan. The most common are the full-automatic Honda Clicks or semi-automatic bikes like the Honda Wave. Unlike upper Myanmar, where most bikes are Chinese, the bikes in Dawei are imported from Thailand. That's another huge plus for southern Myanmar, as they are much more reliable and comfortable. There might also be off-road bikes available, and if you can get your hands on one, I say: go for it. They are much more fun on the rougher dirt tracks.

If you happen to not have any experience with motorbikes or perhaps are traveling as a family, but still want to see the beaches, you can borrow a car with a driver for the day. Depending on how far you want to go, you should be able to get one for around 50,000-100,000 Kyats if you negotiate well. All the beaches and pagodas mentioned in this book are accessible by car, so don't worry about that.

However, when researching for this book, I stumbled across some disturbing news. Apparently, the local government in Dawei has recently banned foreigners from renting motorbikes. They deemed it too "dangerous" for tourists to tour the beaches on their own. They also cited a lack of proper driving licenses as a reason for the ban. That's extremely ironic in my opinion, as most locals in Myanmar have never received a driving license, and nobody really cares.

Considering most tourists come to Dawei for beach exploration, this ban has the potential to almost completely ruin businesses that rely on tourism, like hotels, guesthouses and travel agencies. Frankly, it's an incredibly stupid idea. It didn't surprise me that there was a lot of protest against this ban by people working in the tourism sector.

When I did further research into this ban, I found out from a local friend that the foreigners persisted, and continued renting bikes in Dawei, with the ban not being adequately enforced. The only action the government seems to have taken is to shut down the rental business 'Focus'. Everything else is "business as usual". Good news for you, as there's no need to cancel your Dawei beach trip. Just ask around, and you will find someone willing to rent out his motorbike. An ideal place for that is always your hotel lobby. Hotels and guesthouses are usually well connected to the people renting out bikes. If you have a motorbike driving license in your home country, you should get an international license to be safe.

Once you venture out of Dawei, you have an abundance of places you can visit. The most famous beach is Maungmakan. This beach is extremely popular, especially with the locals from Dawei and the surrounding areas. There are some hotels and even a resort here. The nearby restaurants serve fantastic fish, crab, shrimp and an assortment of other seafood. There are a lot of fishermen in the Dawei area, so whatever you order is freshly caught and comes straight from the Andaman Sea. Maungmakan is an excellent place to pass some time, but it's not the most scenic beach, as it's relatively developed. It's still interesting to observe the people and learn a thing or two about how they spend a day on the beach. There are worse ways to spend an evening than taking a walk on the southern end of the beach (that part is the most scenic) and enjoying the sunset, before having a delicious seafood dinner in one of the restaurants. If you like taking pictures, I recommend climbing one of the small rocky areas just a few meters off the beach. They allow for beautiful views on the beach and the hills in the backcountry.

The last accommodation towards the north is called DDPC Bungalows - we spent a few nights there on our first trip to Dawei. As I consider myself more knowledgeable about this area now, I'd recommend you don't stay in this accommodation. Although the name might make you think of something fancy, it's just a bunch of very basic bungalows that remind you of the cheapest category guesthouses you find anywhere around the country. It's clear that the owners don't put any love into this sleepy hotel. Everything looks a bit unkept. The beach isn't particularly scenic here either. Plus, the place is owned by shady "DDPC" (Dawei Development Public Company), a cooperation that has several big projects in the Dawei area such as gasoline stations and a shopping mall. It's better to spend your money on smaller, family-owned businesses.

Once you get past this "resort", you will have the beach for yourself. From here on out it is pretty much wilderness. Maungmakan Beach is enormous, so if you are into long beach walks this is a brilliant place. If you walk all the way up to the northern tip, you will reach a lagoon that separates Maungmakan and Nabule beach. Nabule is the beach that is likely going to be entirely ruined by a huge seaport project. Even from the northern tip of Maungmakan, you can see some of the development.

Maungmakan Beach is undoubtedly a marvelous start for your Dawei adventure, however, if you really want to start exploring, you will have to head elsewhere. If you continue south from Maungmakan, you will eventually reach the stunning Myaw Yit Pagoda. It's around 30-45 minutes on a bike, with decent road conditions. It's situated on a small island that is connected to the mainline with a bridge, and from here you have a beautiful 360° view on the surrounding coastline.

On the way from Maungmakan to Myaw Yit, you will find several other beaches that are almost completely deserted. You'll pass a beach when you're travelling the last few meters to Myaw Yit which is especially worth visiting. Some people call it San Maria Beach, but I don't think it has an official name yet. At the very end of the beach, you will find a small fishing village. If you are curious as to how the fishermen live and work, you can check it out – it's quite interesting. There are also road-side sugar cane stalls there. Fresh sugar cane juice is a great refreshment when you are tired of the heat and the dust of the roads. Maungmakan, Myaw Yit and the area in-between make for a fantastic day-trip and serve as an ideal preparation for what awaits you further south on the Launglon Peninsula.

Writing about this area gives me a bittersweet feeling. My wife and I originally planned to open our own guesthouse at the edge of the village known as "Kampani". When we moved there to start building the house, something almost unbelievable happened. The local monks (belonging to the now-outlawed nationalist group Ma Ba Tha) decided that they would not accept us living in the village because they suspected my wife (a Christian) of trying to secretly build a church that would divert the villagers away from Buddhism. To achieve their goal of religious purity, they agitated the entire population of Kampani against us and forced us to leave. It was bizarre to experience how powerful these firebrand monks can be. From one day to another we went from warmly welcomed neighbors to ostracized outcast no one wanted to talk to anymore.

Of course, all of this was illegal, but in Myanmar the rule of law is often just an afterthought. As a result of the backlash he faced for letting us stay, the village administrator, at whose house we lived during the time, also left the village shortly after. It's sad how corrupted many Buddhist monks in Myanmar have become and how little they seem to care about the original teachings of the Buddha. The problem of facing this religious extremism is plaguing most of the developers of accommodation projects on the Launglon peninsula. On the one hand it keeps the beaches undeveloped, which is beneficial in many ways, but on the other hand it also stops the local people from profiting from some much-needed development.

Once you are done exploring Maungmakan and the surrounding area, it's time to go to the more remote places. The real adventure starts when you turn left after crossing the Dawei river, as the number of beaches you can explore here is almost endless. It would be impossible to cover every one of them in this book, and therefore I am going to focus on my personal favorites.

When you drive south on the main road, you will eventually pass Launglon, the sleepy capital of the township. Most of the administrative offices are located here but other than a few shops and restaurants there is little reason to make a stop. Driving further south, you will eventually reach a stretch of cliffs. From here you have beautiful views towards the Dawei river flowing into the Andaman Sea - another perfect opportunity for photographers. After passing the cliffs the atmosphere and feel of the surroundings changes a little. Everything starts to feel a bit more laid back and relaxed. Not far from here is a village called Aut Kyauk Wat; remember the name because this village is significant. It acts as the starting point to two remarkable beaches.

One of them is called Grandfather Beach or, Popo Kyauk. The beach can be easily reached from the fishing village, Nyau Pyin, which is only a short distance from Aut Kyauk Wat. When you reach the top of the hill that separates Nyau Pyin and Grandfather Beach, a real revelation awaits you. The first glance down towards the ocean reveals a sheer, endless stretch of silver sand; for me, Grandfather Beach is the most beautiful beach I have ever been to. It's gigantic, and apart from one hotel development project right at the beginning of the beach, it's completely deserted.

Then, at the end of Grandfather Beach, there is a gorgeous turquoise lagoon: combined with the hills in the background, the view is just stunning. The beauty is simply breathtaking and is almost too much for the human mind to process. Fortunately, though there are usually a few people next to the hill where the cars and motorbikes stop, virtually no one ever goes all the way to the lagoon. The sense of the striking wilderness in this spectacular location is truly amazing. Take a moment to sit under a palm tree for a while, and you're almost guaranteed to awaken your inner Robinson Crusoe. In reality, words cannot do it justice; you will have to see for yourself. I can assure you, unless you completely despise beaches, you will be dazzled.

Completely deserted, yet stunning and accessible beaches? *Only in Myanmar!*

The vista is so beautiful that some of the foreign visitors have decided to stay overnight on the beach in previous years. Unfortunately, as with everything that is a bit too fun, the local authorities put an end to it. However, there's no doubt that some people still try their luck. Even though I haven't tried it myself wild camping at one of the remote beaches in the Launglon peninsula is undoubtedly one of the most intense, raw ways to experience true nature. If you decide to try it for yourself, please be as discreet as possible so no one notices you and you don't run into any trouble.

The second beach next to Aut Kyauk Wat is called Paradise Beach. Here you can find the only licensed accommodation on the entire Launglon Peninsula (Myanmar Paradise Beach Bungalows). It's a tricky, narrow dirt ride from the village Aut Kyauk Wat but once you get to the ocean, it's absolute heaven. You can easily spend several days here just relaxing under the palm trees. The bungalows are basic but comfortable, and decently priced.

The beach itself is not as stunning as Grandfather Beach, but it's still superb. Outside the resort area, it's almost always deserted. Now and then some locals come to visit the beach, but if you walk five minutes to the left or the right of the bungalows, you'll have the whole beach to yourself. Currently, only ten bungalows are available, so even if the place is fully booked, it's not crowded at all. If you are into lazy days at the beach and like to get away from the stress of everyday life for a while, this place is utterly perfect. I can recommend checking out the village food in Aut Kyauk Wat instead of eating in the beach restaurant every day; it's cheap and can be delicious. Some of the villagers also sell seasonal fruit in front of their homes next to the main road - don't miss it.

As with any place in Myanmar, you won't have to go far to get to an impressive pagoda. The most stunning one in this area is called Shin Maw Pagoda. This pagoda is situated on the southern tip and feels a little like the end of the world. It's a popular destination for locals and travelers alike. Although the pagoda itself is nothing special, the view over the Andaman Sea is quite spectacular.

To get here, you need to follow the main road; it ends right at the entrance to the pagoda. Keep in mind that it's a pretty long drive from Dawei (around 2-3 hours), so make sure you're adequately prepared. Shortly before you arrive at the Shin Maw pagoda, you pass the so-called Horseshoe Bay; there is an abandoned bungalow resort there and a restaurant, but little else. It's not the most remarkable beach but still worth checking out as it's right next to the main road. It's completely deserted, you are almost guaranteed to have the place to yourself.

To get the most out of your experience, you should keep a few things in mind. I advise you to check your rental bike properly before starting your rides. It needs to be in good shape because having a mechanical breakdown is an excellent way to ruin a day. Check the overall condition of the bike by riding around Dawei for a while, putting extra attention on the brakes and tires. Always wear a helmet and on longer rides, a thin, long-sleeved shirt for sun protection. Sometimes there is quite some distance between the villages, so make sure you don't run out of petrol. The narrow roads that lead from the main road to the beaches usually go through wilderness, so fill up your bike before you head out into the unknown.

Also, make sure you leave the shores before sunset. The dirt tracks are difficult enough to navigate during the day with plenty of bright sunlight; riding them at night is something you don't want to do. Make sure you drive slowly and carefully. If you deem a section of the road to be too dangerous, then don't hesitate to continue on foot. Always remember the most crucial aspect is to arrive safely, no matter how long it takes.

In Myanmar, women traditionally go swimming with their clothes on. That is why I don't advise women to hang around the beach in a bikini, as people will stare at you, and the attention can be very uncomfortable. There are sometimes groups of village children playing on the beaches, and they'll often come and greet you. There is nothing for you to worry about; they just want to have some fun. Dress modestly when driving through villages and be respectful towards any religious places and monks. That means not touching any monks, and not going into a pagoda compound without decent clothes. This is especially important for women. Be friendly, smile and don't haggle too much when you are in remote places.

One thing you should always carry with you is enough water and some snacks. The beaches are usually deserted, so if you run out of water, you may have to cut your time at the beach short. It's not like you have a lot of fancy restaurants you can go to in this part of the country, but keep in mind that the only ATMs in this area are in Dawei. Bring enough cash if you plan on spending several days at the beaches in the south of the Launglon Peninsula.

13. Myanmar's Amazing Teashops

Oh yes, Myanmar food; it's a bit of an ambivalent topic when you are talking to Myanmar travelers. A debate you can frequently hear among other travelers is that the food is too oily, bland and generally not as good as the food in neighboring Thailand, India or China. I don't necessarily disagree. There is a reason why there are so few Myanmar restaurants outside the country. The food is indeed often oily, and it's harder to find good food in Myanmar than in Thailand, for example. But with some experience, the food in Myanmar can be just as good and interesting as anywhere else. What matters is that you know your spots and what dishes to go for. On the positive side, the food in Myanmar is extraordinarily diverse and varies significantly from region to region. There is a near endless list of dishes and snacks that you can try out.

One thing that you should not miss are Myanmar's teashops. Not only are they unique and unlike the breakfast places you might have already experienced in other South-East Asian countries, they are also an integral part of Myanmar culture, and serve not only as a place to fill your belly but also, and maybe just as importantly, meet up and have a chat.

As I already mentioned in the Mohinga chapter, the breakfasts served in hotels and guesthouses are often very underwhelming and can be straight-up boring. You can eat fried eggs, toast and strawberry jam at home, so there is no need to eat a worse version of your standard breakfast when you are in Myanmar. Head out of your hotel and dive into Myanmar's own breakfast culture instead. The omnipresent teashops are an excellent place to experience this. Many people in Myanmar, especially the ones living in the cities, start each day here by having breakfast and chatting with their colleagues or friends.

The term "teashop" is misleading, however. Yes, tea is getting served here, but Myanmar teashops are so much more. They serve a variety of fried snacks, coffee, tea, juices and often also rice and noodle dishes. Anything people eat for breakfast in Myanmar can be found here. The leading teashops in central Mandalay and Yangon can be huge establishments, serving hundreds of hungry customers each morning. From my personal experience, the bigger and busier teashops rarely serve up lousy food. After all, there's a reason they're so popular. They also often have menus which makes ordering much easier for tourists, and quite often, they also offer the widest choice. The smaller teashops, often family-run businesses, aren't necessarily worse but they are a lot more hit and miss than the larger ones. They usually specialize in a limited number of dishes, so you won't be able to get everything you might want in them. Owing to these reasons, my advice is to choose the sizeable, busier venues, just to make sure the quality of food is excellent.

Many teashops can't be found online and aren't mentioned in guidebooks, so you might have to ask around a little. Alternatively, you can take a motorbike taxi and ask to be taken to a big teashop. If your hotel is in a central area, just walking around will also do the trick, as teashops are everywhere in Myanmar.

Apart from just having breakfast, visiting a teashop is an experience in and of itself. In my opinion, you absolutely cannot come to Myanmar and never go to a teashop. That would be almost as bad as visiting Yangon but skipping Shwedagon Pagoda. A busy teashop is a truly fantastic sight. Just observing what's going on around you is a real experience. I have lived in Myanmar for several years, yet I still find it impressive how adept and organized the staff at these big teashops are. No offense to waiters in the west, but none of them could serve as many tables as fast these guys. It boggles the mind how much work they do every day and how little they get paid for it. Most of them come from poor village families, skip school and do all this crazy work for only around $60, and a place to sleep. No vacations, no days off. The way they are constantly rushing from table to table, shouting incoming orders towards the cooks, picking up ready dishes and bringing them to the tables in record speeds is almost a form of art. At the same time, they are listening to the orders that the customers shout across several tables and clean up after they've left. Through all this, they almost always manage to get the orders right and rarely forget something. Even though they get little recognition for the job they do, these guys are truly the heroes of everyday life. Their multi-tasking skills, shrewdness and stamina are amazing.

Considering the time you will be able to spend in Myanmar is likely limited, it is going to be close to impossible to try out everything that the many teashops around Myanmar's bigger and smaller towns offer up. Even after living in Myanmar for years, I still discover new dishes every so often. Despite the diversity, there are some classics that you should try at least once. First of all, the tea. In Myanmar, people drink two types of tea. One is the unsweetened green tea that you can usually find in thermos flasks on tables of restaurants. This tea is actually free, and you can drink as much as you want. Then there is the sweet tea that is served in tea shops. It's a black tea mixed with condensed milk. Depending on how sweet you like it you can either order "La Phe Ye Pohn Mahn" (regular sweet tea) or "La Phe Ye Kyo Sain" (very sweet).

Then we have the deep-fried snacks. The perfect complement to sweet tea is called "Ih Kyar Kway", it's a breadstick made of flour and can be dipped into the tea, if you like. "Paun Mok Kyaw" is another satisfying dish. It's French toast, Burmese style. The difference when compared to the French version is that sugar and condensed milk get poured over it before it's served. Yes, it is as unhealthy as it sounds. "Pa La Ta" is also a classic, it's a flatbread that is inspired by Indian cuisine. It's often eaten with sugar sprinkled on top of it or with a hearty side dish made of mashed beans. Samosa can also be found in Myanmar tea shops. They are usually stuffed with potatoes and eaten with a delicious tamarind sauce. Some people also like to eat them as "Samosa Thoke", which is a salad of mashed Samosas and rice.

Admittedly, your doctor would not approve of any of this. All these snacks are loaded with fat, white flour and sugar; actual calorie bombs that even manage to make American fast food seem healthy. But hey, you are likely to only be in Myanmar for a few weeks, so a bit of sinning is fine. You have the perfect excuse anyways, as eating all these deep-fried snacks is a kind of food exploration after all. And everyone knows, if you are a real explorer, you sometimes need to take some "extreme" measures, to get where you want to go. Having a breakfast that is pushing you close to a heart attack is something found *only in Myanmar.* The good news for your cardiovascular health is that there are also less unhealthy breakfast options available.

You can have a dish called "Bamar Ta Min Kyaw". It's fried rice but without the usual selection of meat and vegetables. It's often eaten with whole garlic and chili and has a very natural taste to it - it's one of my favorites and is a staple for breakfast in Myanmar. If you are more into noodles, you have several other options, one of them being "Nan Gyi Thoke". This noodle dish is a true classic for breakfast. It consists of thick rice noodles and a special curry that can include meat. It's often garnished with slices of boiled egg, lemon and sliced onions. Out of the dishes available in Myanmar, it's one of my favorites. The way 'it's prepared varies a lot, so no two bowls of "Nan Gyi Thoke" are ever the same. "Ohn No Khao Swé" is another classic. It's a dish consisting of noodles and a delicious thick coconut-chicken broth. The coconut milk gives it a slight sweetness, which sets it apart from most other noodle dishes found in Myanmar.

One thing that you should keep in mind is that in many teashops the deep-fried snacks like "Ih Kyaw Kway" are only available until around 8.30am. That means that you will have to get there early if you don't want to miss out. Noodles and rice-based dishes are generally available throughout the day. Some teashops, however, are only open during the morning hours. If you want to visit a teashop, breakfast is undoubtedly the meal you should be going for.

Often you can see the staff prepare dishes at the side of, or even in the front of the teashop. The reason for that is they have to make big fires to heat the oil that is used for frying all the delicious snacks inside hulking iron pots.

Obviously, the kitchen is not a suitable place for that. The advantage of this is that it makes it easy to get an idea of what food is available when you arrive at the teashop.

One last thing that I want to share is that writing all this while being thousands of kilometers away from the next teashop is borderline masochistic. Just the thought of all these glorious snacks makes my mouth water. What I wouldn't give to sit down and order a beautiful selection of tea, "Nan Gyi Thoke" and some "Pa La Ta".

14. Sources for more research

All the links you find in this chapters are compelled in the Facebook-Page of this book. I hope that will make using them easier for you. You can find the link to it on the last page of this book.

Myanmar train travel

While researching for this book, I found the website *myanmartrainticket.com*. Apparently, it's a travel agent that can buy train tickets on your behalf. Ordering tickets online would make using Myanmar's trains a lot easier, but I cannot confirm whether or not the service is legit or if it works as promised. The website offers lots of information regardless, so give it a try.

Another good source of information is *www.seat61.com/Burma.htm.* You can find anything from prices to train schedules here.

Mohinga

A great piece of information is this blog: *tastingtable.com/dine/national/mohinga-burmese-soup-burma-superstar?utm_source=tt&utm_medium=email&utm_campaign=normal*

If you want to cook Mohinga yourself, several recipes can be found online. This is one of the best ones I've found so far: *196flavors.com/burma-mohinga/*

Sa Done Waterfall in Kachin state

Part of its allure is that the waterfall is not mentioned in any guidebooks. It's not even marked on Google Maps. The only help I can give you are the waterfall's coordinates:

25°21'36.7"N 97°47'34.3"E

The best preparation for the trip is to search for the coordinates in Google Maps (satellite version) and follow the road back to Washawng, Wainmaw and Myitkyina. That way, you get an idea of the terrain and will not feel completely lost when being out on the road. Of course, using Google Earth works for this as well.

Beer stations

Read up on the first Myanmar microbrewery here: *burbrit.com* and here: *frontiermyanmar.net/en/the-microbrew-revolution-comes-to-yangon.*

Mandalay pagoda climbing

When you are in Mandalay and need a motorbike, I can recommend the services of my friend Zach. He runs *mandalaymotorbike*.com and is a great guy. You can rent the usual Chinese 125cc bikes or bigger 250cc Hondas from his shop. All the bikes are well maintained and generally in much better shape than the rental bikes you will find elsewhere in Myanmar. It doesn't matter if you plan on making a big multi-day road trip or just require something to get you around Mandalay, he is the man for you.

As mentioned before, I also recommend Amitav Ghosh's The Glass Palace. It's a great book covering the British invasion of Burma and the end of the **Konbaung Dynasty** in **Mandalay**. It also includes the period during the Second World War and after. It's a novel, and I am not sure how accurately it reflects history, but even if it has some weaknesses, it's still a great way to familiarize yourself with the interesting times of British Burma, and how the second world war affected Myanmar. Part of the story plays out in Mandalay and Yangon. I randomly stumbled over a copy of the book in a small bookshop in Myitkyina. I didn't know anything about the author of the book, but it was a great find and gave me many fascinating hours of reading.

Buddhism in Myanmar

Buddhanet.net is an excellent website for free Buddhist resources. You find a link to the book Snow in the Summer here: _buddhanet.net/pdf_file/jotleeds.pdf_

And the book "On the Path to Freedom" can be found here: _buddhanet.net/pdf_file/path-free.pdf_

The full text of the Time magazine article about Wirathu can be found here: _colombotelegraph.com/index.php/full-text-of-the-banned-time-story-the-face-of-buddhist-terror/_

Friendliness

Read up on what others think about the people of Myanmar.

„But it's Myanmar that takes the congeniality award. The people are charming and friendly. And I would even venture to say that they are the friendliest we've met in our travels anywhere in the world.“ – from the blog: twowanderingsoles.com/blog/how-myanmar-is-different-from-any-country-we-have-visited-in-the-world

"The friendliness of the Burmese people was extraordinary."[...] "When I think about my time in Myanmar, I picture all the smiling faces that I met on my journey:"[...] "The positive energy, the warm feelings, the sense of appreciation – it's all priceless – and it blew me away." from the blog: itchyfeetonthecheap.com/2016/09/09/myanmar-friendliest-people-country/

"The Burmese people were a highlight of our trip – friendly, welcoming, and often very excited to meet us. We were smiled at and chatted to, pointed and waved at, and occasionally hysterically laughed at (that may have been our attempts to speak Burmese)." – from the blog: neverendingvoyage.com/35-random-observations-about-burma-myanmar/

Betel nut

There is plenty of information on the internet regarding the health effects of chewing the betel nut. The most interesting information can be found here: *thahara.com/blog/betel-nut-in-myanmar*

Colonial architecture

There are plenty of blogs about Myanmar's colonial architecture. A great one I stumbled across when researching for this book is goingcolonial.com/top-10-colonial-buildings-yangon-myanmar/. It lists the most beautiful colonial buildings and offers pictures and information.

If you are looking to get inspired go for one of the picture databases like this one: *pinterest.de/palethitsar/colonial-buildings-in-myanmar/*

The website of the Commonwealth War Graves Commission is a good source of information for the Taukkyan War Cemetery. Here is the link: *www.cwgc.org/find-a-cemetery/cemetery/92001/RANGOON%20WAR%20CEMETERY*

The blog *malaysia-traveller.com/Maymyo-Christian-Cemetery.html* offers the only information regarding the Pyin U Lwin war cemetery I could find. It's a fascinating read, regardless of whether you plan to visit the cemetery or not.

Myanmar's classical cars

There isn't much research you can do on these, you simply have to experience them for yourself. However, I did find an interesting blog which taught me a few things I didn't know myself. It's mostly about the blue Mazdas and other vehicles like the Myanmar Jeeps, but it's still a great resource. You can find it here: *bestsellingcarsblog.com/2013/06/myanmar-the-old-chevrolet-and-mazda-trucks-from-burma/*

Beach hunting in Dawei

The best source of information for Dawei's beaches is a guide written by a guy called Stephen, on his extremely informative blog. He is known all around Dawei for his research, and I have seen his guides printed out in a guesthouse before. Your best bet is just to bookmark it in your browser. It's not an exaggeration to say that without his guide, most people wouldn't have a clue these beaches even exist, let alone know how to get there. Here is the link:

https://myohmyanmar.wordpress.com/2014/03/14/no-need-to-archipelago-try-the-beaches-on-the-dawei-peninsula/

Another useful piece of information is the website *southernmyanmar.com*, it covers all of southern Myanmar and not just Dawei. Unlike Stephen's guide, it also lists businesses operating in the area. There is a good list of hotels, guesthouses and tour guides available.

Even though I have never used their services, I have heard a lot of good things about Life Seeing Tours. This travel agency operates out of Myeik and is the best place for more organized tours. Perfect for people who don't want to explore entirely on their own. You can find plenty of information about their services on their website *lifeseeingtours.com*.

Teashops

There isn't much reading you have to do before visiting a Myanmar teashop, but if you like doing extensive research, you can go through the blogs: *wanderingwheatleys.com/best-tea-shops-in-mandalay-myanmar/* and *dustinmain.com/home/anatomy-of-a-burmese-teashop-myanmar*. Both of these blogs offer some information as to what teashops are like, including pictures of some of the most popular dishes.

If you want to go for the cream of the crop, you can find a list of the best teashops in Yangon here: *mmtimes.com/news/top-10-tea-shops-yangon.html.* This is certainly enough to get your mouth watering. In fact, just writing this makes me hungry again, God damn it. Why can't someone open a Myanmar teashop in Germany?

15. Final words

Dear reader,

I'd like to take a moment to personally thank you for reading my humble book. I sincerely hope you've enjoyed reading about all the unique experiences, that I've explored within these pages. It would give me a great sense of pride if this book was inspirational enough to convince you to take your own adventure, and to discover the Golden Country for yourself.
If you have decided to journey to this gorgeous nation, I truly wish you an unforgettable trip. If not, then I hope you've at least learned something about Myanmar while reading this book, and that you can take away knowledge of this country's more unique aspects, rich culture and vibrant history.

Thank you.

ကျေးဇူးတင်ပါသည်

Kyay Su Tin Ba De

Want to share your own experiences?

Visit my Facebook-Page!

facebook.com/OnlyMyanmar